ADVANCE PRAISE FOR

Becoming a Global Audience

"Juluri's study has the great merit of being rooted in a political-economic analysis of the Indian culture industry and a sophisticated (but never simplistic or populist) account of reception. His study has solid empirical foundations and theoretical elegance; both threads weave through this book like a beautifully constructed combination of rhythm and melody.

As music and culture have gone global, so has theory; and while the internationalization of musical culture has been a mixed blessing (as Juluri shows), the impact of local and global studies on cultural studies has been all to the good. If there was ever a time for a postcolonialist—as opposed to a postmodern—approach to media audiences, it is now. On this promise, Juluri delivers.

In both senses of the term, this book advances our understanding of popular culture on a truly global scale."

—Andrew Goodwin, Professor & Chair, Department of Media Studies, University of San Francisco.

"Vamsee Juluri's book is a superb example of how globalized mass media, such as transnational television, shape the subjectivities, identities, and yearnings of men and women in particular locations. At the same time that this study enables us to understand the configuration of global political-economic and cultural fields of power, it also brings to our attention how these are implicated in the everyday lives of people. A lucid and elegant book, it is a must-read for scholars of globalization, transnational cultural studies, and mass media."

—Purnima Mankekar, Associate Professor of Anthropology, Stanford University; author of Screening Culture, Viewing Politics.

Becoming a Global Audience

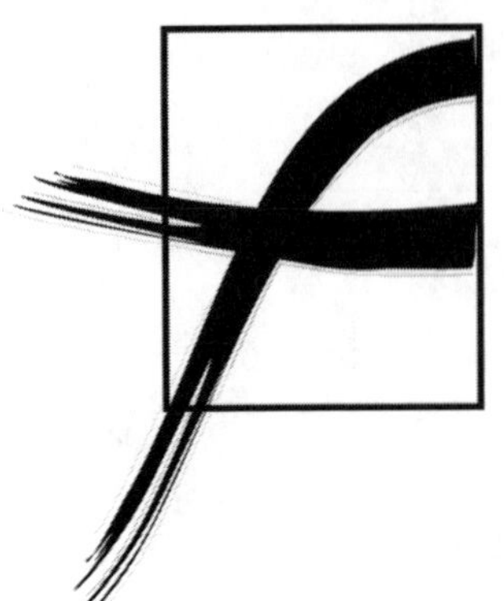

Intersections in Communications and Culture

Global Approaches and Transdisciplinary Perspectives

Cameron McCarthy and Angharad N. Valdivia
General Editors

Vol. 2

PETER LANG
New York • Washington, D.C./Baltimore • Bern
Frankfurt am Main • Berlin • Brussels • Vienna • Oxford

Vamsee Juluri

Becoming a Global Audience

Longing and Belonging in Indian Music Television

PETER LANG
New York • Washington, D.C./Baltimore • Bern
Frankfurt am Main • Berlin • Brussels • Vienna • Oxford

Library of Congress Cataloging-in-Publication Data

Juluri, Vamsee.
Becoming a global audience: longing and belonging
in Indian music television / Vamsee Juluri.
p. cm. — (Intersections in communications and culture; vol. 2)
Includes bibliographical references and index.
1. Music television—India. I. Title. II. Series.
PN1992.8.M87 J85 791.45'6—dc21 2001034691
ISBN 0-8204-5579-2
ISSN 1528-610X

Bibliographic information published by **Die Deutsche Bibliothek**.
Die Deutsche Bibliothek lists this publication in the "Deutsche
Nationalbibliografie"; detailed bibliographic data is available
on the Internet at http://dnb.ddb.de/.

Cover concept by Anand Kamalakar
Cover design by Lisa Barfield

The paper in this book meets the guidelines for permanence and durability
of the Committee on Production Guidelines for Book Longevity
of the Council of Library Resources.

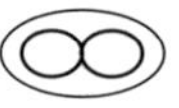

275 Seventh Avenue, 28th Floor, New York, NY 10001
www.peterlangusa.com

Printed in the United States of America

CONTENTS

ACKNOWLEDGMENTS

My first homage is to Justin Lewis, for enabling the meeting of audience research, cultural studies, and globalization in this book. As my Ph.D. advisor, Justin provided support and clarity that helped me negotiate the demands placed on this project by the sheer scale of the satellite television boom in India on the one hand and the institutional imperatives of the academy on the other.

I also thank R. Radhakrishnan who blessed this title and provided strong friendship, guidance, and support. Sut Jhally was and remains an inspiration. Henry Geddes spelled out the big picture on globalization with eloquence and insight. Dr. Lucy Nguyen and the United Asia Learning Resource Center at the University of Massachusetts provided a support network that made much of my research and writing possible.

For support and valuable insights during the research for this book, I thank the faculty and students of the Department of Mass Communication at the University of Hyderabad. I am especially grateful to Dean B. P. Sanjay, Vinod Pavarala, Mr. Manvi, Thirumal, and C.V.S. Sarma.

An earlier phase of the writing of this book was helped in no small manner by the friendship and support of John Shotter, Sheila McNamee, Jack Lannamann, Pat Daley, Beverly James, Josh Meyrowitz, and especially John Erni.

This book was brought to its completion at the University of San Francisco thanks to the kind support and encouragement of Dean Stanley Nel, Dean Jennifer Turpin, and Andrew Goodwin (and the timely help of Michelle Fremount).

I would also like to thank Angharad Valdivia for insightful guidance in revising this book, and Sophy Craze, for making it possible.

Finally, I offer this book to all my families: my father, Professor J. V. Ramana Rao, and mother, Jamuna; my sister, J.R.M. Sravanthi, the original MTV survivor; B.P.R. Vithal and Seshu Vithal; Sanjaya and Rama Baru; Murali and Nivedita Kumar; and Lakshmi Attha and Kalyan Sagar.

INTRODUCTION

The emergence of the satellite television audience has been an integral part of the experience of contemporary globalization in India and the profound changes in the conditions of existence that this process entails. From a television environment marked by the presence of a single state-owned broadcaster, Doordarshan, India plunged almost instantly into a landscape of privately owned satellite channels. In 1990, a typical TV household in India watched one channel for a few hours every day. A decade later, there were about 37 million households in India watching dozens of cable and satellite (C/S) television channels voraciously. The percentage of those who "rarely watched" TV declined dramatically, even as the number of channels available at all geocultural levels (global, Asian, national, regional, and local) proliferated (Elsham, 2002; Fernandes, 2000; "Couch potatoes on the rise," 1998). The significance of this phenomenon may be appreciated not only in terms of its rapidity and scale but also in the fact that the television audience is an important constitutive site in which globalization is experienced as an immediate, totalizing, and meaningful effect in the contemporary world.

The nature of this effect is not so much in the way of a simple televisual emanation upon attitude, opinion, or behavior, but rather in the fact that there has come into being a set of ways of living in the world—ways that carry the value and weight of community, relationships, and identity—that are attributed coherence, meaning, and a sense of normalcy in direct relation to the specific forms that television has taken under the economic logics of globalization—and under the specific conditions that life itself has acquired under the social logics of globalization. In this book, I describe the rise of music television in India in the 1990s, including the coming of MTV and the promises of representation and national authority that its contents seemed to offer; and situate the music television audience in India as one that has been constructed at the fraught and fragile moment in everyday life where the collapsing worlds of nonmodern sociality and the emerging global relations of modernity fall upon each other.

The picture of the global audience that I invoke in this book is therefore not one of masses of anonymous eyes in the dark fixed upon an American pop music video; it is perhaps better described as a resistive elegy to the appropriation of an Indian sentiment mighty enough to represent the possibility of a global condition by an imperialistic injunction that has fractured the conditions of existence of this sentiment in India (and elsewhere)—even as it claims to be spreading this sentiment to the far corners of earth on the basis of a false sense of reciprocity and symmetry. Music television is perceived by its viewers as offering them a world that represents them in every way; as family members, friends, citizens, and Indians facing the eyes of the rest of the world. This offer, though, has semiotic costs and social consequences: the images and stories of music television around which audiences see themselves as Indians may be accurately characterized as a form of self-orientalism, a process in which Indian music television exoticizes everything it can find in and as India, creating an illusory world in which everything feels like it is still India, but appears as if someone else was looking at it.

In this new India as a global idea, the terms of definition have come from elsewhere, from beyond even the giant media corporations for whom the Indian audience is just another big emerging market. The terms of definition come ultimately from the historical system of cruelty that is the foundation of the global condition. From this perspective, the media and the audience are perhaps best appreciated as the institutional and epistemological legacies respectively of colonialism, and the vision of the self, the nation, and the world that emerges from music television audiences in India embodies a continuing struggle against the enduring brutality that sustains a particular worldview that Davies, Nandy, and Sardar (1993) have described as the "oculus mundi," or the "eye of the world (conqueror)." Becoming global, as a music television audience, under these terms, is one more way of keeping cool under conditions of conquest.

While it would not be accurate to downplay or dismiss the pleasures and joys of music television in India as nothing more than the victimization of Indian audiences by global media, it is worth the attempt to characterize the moment at which the forces of contemporary global imperialism face off, as it were, against the lingering feelings of community. These feelings, which I have characterized in this book as longing and belonging, are the main meanings that audiences bring to Indian music television in the context of globalization as an everyday experience. Becoming global, for Indian music television audiences, is a process of seeking—sometimes with a false sense of success—recognition of who they believe they really are. Who they believe they really are is not, at least by the parameters of their own definitions, anything like the modern, self-centered, individual subject associated with the discourses of media and consumer culture. Instead, the core value that emerges in this study is one of belonging; the Indian music television audience sees itself in terms of its relational values and identities; and the songs and programs all somehow as expressions of these.

To illustrate, as recently as early 2002, the popular Zee TV film-song based game show *Antakshari*[1] featured a special episode on relationships; and its particular focus was the father-daughter. The participants included three father-daughter teams (two of the daughters were Indian Miss Worlds) and many of the songs used in this episode dealt with the sentiments of fathers and daughters. To anyone who has seen the faces of people who participate in this show (or those who watch it), the resonance it has with Indian people is profoundly obvious. Drawing on the endless reservoir of songs from Indian cinema (with 1,000 feature films a year and an average of seven songs per film, and well over 50 years of existence, the Indian film industry remains an armory of "music videos" that the new television could hardly even hope to match), *Antakshari* is all about participation; not only in the long-familiar joys of singing songs that express everything from family sentiments and nationalistic ideals to prurient juvenilia and nonsense rhymes, but to more recent television-based pleasures of self-recognition and identification, as well. In other words, *Antakshari*, with its unabashed flights of singing is Indian popular expression itself. But it is also about a new world in which there are new discursive demands on these expressions; demands that range from classifying an otherwise amorphous expression of musical joy into cognitive categories and competitive formats to gratuitous genuflections for imagined prides and glories. To illustrate, the sincere daughterly sentiments with which these participants enter the game is anchored, in the age of the global audience, to their particularly contemporary status as beauty pageant winners who are introduced in this show by the host as India's pride, and yes, the pride of the whole world too.

My argument in this book is that this is no simple articulation of nonmodern sentiments and modern discourses. It is an act of war—if not in the terms of discourse, at least in the broader social shifts that accompany these discourses. If music television audiences identify with family ties, they are bringing in their remnants of affections and understandings that have acquired a sad sort of curiousness in their attempts to keep relational values aloft in a world that complicates and confounds the possibilities of their existence. To put it another way, the last decade in India has seen profound changes in social relations, not only in the broader levels of economic and political power, but in the more immediate context of family fragmentations and migrations related to the growing, pressing demands of mobility in every sense. A recent hit song in India was "lift *kara de*" (give me a lift)—a paean to opportunity, advancement, and success. For large portions of the middle classes, economic liberalization has certainly made this happen. This raises the question of "At what cost?," but more precisely, the question of how this cost may be compounded by the popular stories and justifications that have been delivered by media discourses to account for these changes. Music television has brought in images, narratives, and ideologies that in the world of the audience seem to offer a tentative rest from the travails of real-life modernity on families and relationships; however, these discourses are more than a mere explanation; by virtue of their existence in a global, modern, imperialist context, they come with an epistemic brutality that makes them usurp and devour any potential that other, still existing values may have for alternative social vision and action.

To put it another way, music television's genres and conventions call upon the audience to assume certain ways of knowing—not only the meaning of the text, but everything else that is entailed—knowing themselves, and knowing the world. These ways of knowing are directly related to the new globalized forms of production, although much of the sentimentality expressed around these programs goes back to the preglobal television era. I describe the particularities of these ways of knowing in relation to three main themes in this book: knowing how to watch music television, knowing how to watch countdown shows, and knowing how to watch nationalistic music videos. In conclusion, I discuss the broader consequences of what it means to know, or not to (be in the) know. This does not necessarily mean that "meaning" is unidimensional or uniformly accessible to viewers. From my interviews, it is apparent that viewers bring in a lot more to the reading of texts than what is said within them. Conversely, there is also the need to address the many historically new forms and conventions within music television that participants in this study do not necessarily address, but these exist, and have to be accounted for in some manner.

As these issues suggest, this study is an attempt to situate audience studies in a global context and to concurrently recognize postcoloniality as the fundamental condition of the global context. This is a process that entails an engagement with at least two streams in the literature: (1) the debates on international communication and globalization, and particularly the relationship of audience studies to the political-economy approach; and (2) the debates within cultural studies about audiences and reception, particularly in the context of globalization. While I discuss the theoretical positions this study adopts vis-à-vis these debates momentarily, it is useful, at the outset, to outline some empirical aspects of media globalization in India that challenge a simplistic understanding of globalization as "Westernization" or "Americanization" and music television as a harbinger of a uniform and anti-elder "youth culture." As Appadurai and Breckenridge (1996) argue, the experience of global modernity in South Asia cannot be seen as a simple process of "McDonaldization" or "cultural homogenization," especially since the coming of satellite television to India has not been marked by a simple influx of Western programming (Chadha & Kavoori, 2000). Instead, the landscape of music television in India has acquired the hues of hybridity, mixing the songs and sentiments of India's many cinemas with the pop idiom and conventions of American television culture. On global music television channels like MTV and Channel V, on Indian national music television channels like Music Asia, and in extensive film and film music-based programs on national and regional channels, the experience of music television in India presents a depth and complexity as challenging as any question that takes on globalization as its object of study.

Music Television and Youth Culture in India

The advent of satellite television in India in the immediate wake of the Gulf War and the economic liberalization policies of the Indian government in 1991 seemed to herald an impending deluge of American programs, but the enormous growth that took place in the following years assumed a form that has invalidated such a simple assumption. To put it another way, by the mid-1990s, satellite television in India seemed very much "Indian," even if many of the channels were "international" or foreign-owned. The role of music television in this process cannot be understated. In early 1991, the first cable/satellite subscribers in urban upper-class India received a small number of channels, including Star Plus and MTV. This was still the MTV of Western pop music videos, and one especially popular Asian VJ (Nonie). However, by the summer of 1994, satellite television had grown immensely in terms of distribution as well as the number of channels, and MTV went off the Star TV platform, to be replaced by Channel V, a music television channel that seemed strikingly Indian and international at the same time.

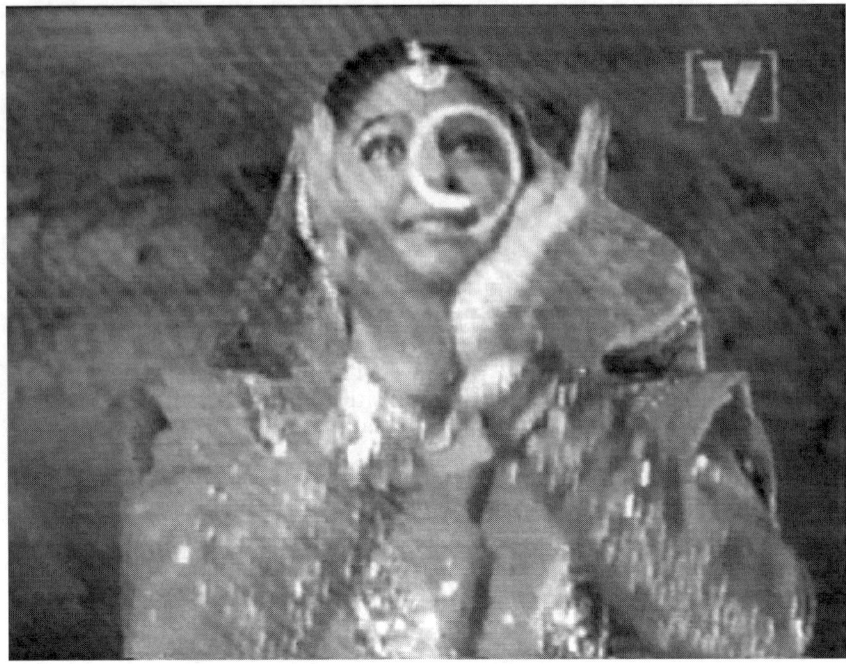

FIGURE 1 A gift from the sky? Music television comes to India. An image from the title sequence of Channel V's Indian Top Ten.

Channel V's entry strategy was "localize or bust" (Hussain, 1997). With Indian film songs, promos featuring Indian street life, multiracial VJs, and a quaint and self-conscious hybrid language mixing English, Hindi, and Indian English, it quickly became the channel on which a whole generation of Indians began to grow up, much as MTV was in the United States in the early 1980s. However, the inscription of generational identity upon Indian audiences by music television did not necessarily imply an anti-parent "youth culture" either. Channel V positioned itself to secure an intergenerational audience rather than an exclusive youth audience, complicating if not belying the evocations of guilt and suspicion that the very notion of "youth culture" has aroused in other contexts (Austin & Willard, 1998). Such concerns about Westernization or youth culture seemed even more confounded when MTV India began operations in 1996, aggressively following a strategy of localization as well.

However, the apparent normalcy of the advent and acceptance of music television in India is a politically fraught one. Although MTV's marketing strategy of localization may not have produced cultural homogeneity in the sense of American content, it also remains to be seen if this has led to what Simon Philo (1999) calls "contestation and challenge" (p. 76) in a socially meaningful manner. It is perhaps more useful to turn to the local site of reception, as Wilson and Dissanayake (1996) have argued, as not simply a resistive binary opposite to the dominant global, but as a more complex site of contestation in which the global enacts dominances and resistances. In addition, even though music television may not have engendered an overtly rebellious youth culture in India, it has still produced both a nascent form of youth culture (premised on the constraints of intergenerational audiences) and to some extent the very idea of youth culture as well.

This may mark the beginning of what Grossberg (1997) describes in the U.S. postwar context as the creation of a marketized "culture of transitions" from what in India would be a weakly defined "transitional culture" in the first place (p. 85). Channel V, for instance, initially positioned itself as being "For the young and young at heart," and described itself to advertisers as a "youth channel in attitude, but a family channel in demographics" (Hussain, 1997). The simultaneous appeals to young and old by Indian music television channels, however, do mark a departure from earlier programming strategies. As one commentator has observed, this transformation in Indian television may be best described as a move from "worshipping senility" (on Doordarshan) to "worshipping juvenility" (Shah, 1997). In other words, even if the coming of global television to India did not mean a simple influx of Western youth culture, it has resulted in a broad transformation across the rapidly growing mediascape that is manifested as a strange worship of youthful exuberance that still has a somewhat halfhearted place in the pantheon for family and nation.

If the content of music television has not overtly encouraged generational rebellion or political engagement in any serious manner, it is also worth noting that music television has not been met by political opposition or condemnation in a sustained manner either. The few examples of "controversy" surrounding music television in the last decade include objections raised in the Indian Parliament to MTV's use of the colors of the Indian flag for its logo in 1998, and more recently, Channel V being charged by the police for having a couple of participants on its program *V Dares You* streak across a street in Mumbai. Although "culture" has indeed become a political slogan in India in recent years, the pervasive presence of much of what is seen on Indian television has surprisingly been largely ignored, if not occasionally sanctioned. After all, it would seem, much of what is seen in India is now produced by and for Indians, as it were. While Channel V and MTV India have vied with one another in appearing more "Indian," there were also other music television channels and programs that appeared by the mid-1990s that were largely Indian in content and ownership.

However, the true import of the rise of music television in India extends far beyond the occasional moments of confrontation or controversy. What is more important, especially from the perspective of audience research, is the quiet turning into normalcy of everything that has happened and continues to happen on music television in India. In the early 1990s, satellite television may have seemed new and slightly perplexing. In 1997, at the time I conducted the interviews for this study, everything seemed normal. It is this apparent sense of normalcy in music television that is perhaps the core of the media effect—in a broad sense—that globalization and satellite television have entailed in India. One way of appreciating the potency of normalization[2] would be to simply list out some representative examples of what seemingly passes for normalcy, or "entertainment" in Indian music television.

In a dating game show, a male contestant tries to impress his prospective date by saying that his favorite hobbies are sky diving and bungee jumping (not necessarily the most popular or affordable of pastimes in India). On Sony TV's popular music countdown *Take Five*, a young man in a dance club shouts obscenities at his parents. Promos on music television routinely ridicule working-class people, while music videos show modern-day princesses benevolently alighting from yachts and smiling at poor island children. Images of the poor and working class also bolster top ten shows while "public" shows featuring impromptu street interviews claim to be of and for and by the people. Religious imagery forms a new urban ethnic chic; saffron-clad rappers chant "I'm an Indian," while teenagers on motorbikes with bumper stickers of Hindu gods cavort to pop versions of traditional religious songs. In some other music videos, children fantasize about adult women in video game arcades, and strive remarkably to appear cute in otherwise precocious situations. All the while, music videos—and film songs in the age of music videos—celebrate being Indian in relation to a somewhat morally confused West (that is still deemed to have the competence to recognize Indian greatness): "Made in India," "I love my India," "East or West, India is the Best."

In short, the sudden and sweeping transformation of television in India has resulted in an intense profusion of stories and images that elude simple description but yet press the question of what it all may mean—especially within the ambitious terms of the notion of globalization. If one inference may be drawn from these examples, it is that a simplistic interpretation of globalization as cultural homogenization (with the attendant entreaties to the "preservation" of cultural "differences") is inaccurate; and so is the conflation of MTV with the spread of a uniform, anti-elder youth culture. These limitations, however, do not by any means imply that satellite television has not had an effect in terms of "globalizing" its audiences. Instead, it is more useful to recognize the limitations of traditional debates, particularly in terms of the still inadequate engagement with questions about audiences and reception in the broader debates about media globalization. In the following section, I outline my theoretical position about audiences in relation to the conceptualization of audiences (or lack thereof) in the debates on media globalization first, and then examine in greater depth the tensions and trajectories in cultural studies approaches to audiences that characterize the moment that cultural studies and globalization confront one another.

Globalization and Audiences

The contemporary phase of media globalization has been usefully addressed in terms of its political-economy more recently by Herman and McChesney (1997), who argue that the global march of capitalist media corporations in a deregulatory political climate is leading to privatization, commercialization, and a weakening of the public sphere as a resource and forum for political participation. The political economy of global media is clearly all that Herman and McChesney say it is, but there is much more that needs to be understood in terms of the experience of media globalization—and especially the political nature of this experience.

Such a sociologically grounded approach is apparent in the work of Tomlinson (1999), who vividly describes the nature of "mediated experience" under modernity and portrays globalization as a process involving complex and deep social connections between people and activities across spaces and times. The key question that Tomlinson's approach cannot address, however, is the meaningfulness of these experiences for those who are situated within them—the question of culture as meaning. Although, like Waters (1995), Tomlinson locates culture and globalization as mutually constitutive, he does not necessarily foreground the relevance of culture in terms of the meanings that audiences may make of their mediated experiences.

It would seem therefore that the study of globalization and media needs to turn its attention to the media audience, not merely as a commercially constructed aggregate of viewers, or partially disembodied subjects of global modernity, but as the point at which media are made meaningful and effectivized. It is also worth noting in this context the somewhat divergent trajectories that audience studies and studies of global media have followed in the path—with audience studies somehow becoming associated with cultural studies in the West and global media studies (or international communication in more traditional circles) following a largely political-economic approach. This divergence, as I have argued elsewhere (Juluri, 1998) is more a matter of the geopolitics of the academy and knowledge-production rather than any useful distinction, and these are two areas of media studies that merit closer interaction.

The juxtaposition of these approaches is important not only because of the need to overcome what is arguably an artificial distinction, but also because the concerns of international communication scholars and those of audience scholars have often been posed as contradictory, as Roach (1997) shows in her comprehensive reading of the debate. It would seem that the absolutely legitimate concern about the growing monopolization of media and cultural production by a small number of powerful and wealthy corporations with tremendous transnational resources—a condition that Schiller (1991, p. 13) characterizes as "not yet the post-imperialist era"—necessarily negates the relevance of how audiences actually negotiate the meanings of the messages produced by these media corporations and that these meanings may have some kind of broad social and cultural implications. Conversely, even merely raising the question of audience readings of media texts seems to signal a belief in the unfettered ability of audiences to resist dominant meanings; and even some of the most sophisticated critiques of global media and cultural imperialism end up saying that audience studies cannot but confirm audience resistance over media power (Tomlinson, 1991).

This polarization may be worked around by turning to a brief review of how audiences have been conceptualized in media studies. The rise of the "meaning paradigm" and the broader inputs of British Cultural Studies since the 1970s may be taken as one seminal moment on the basis of which much useful contemporary theorizing is taking place. The specific "breaks" that this moment effected with the traditional American version of mass communication research until that point (Hall, 1982), and the rich and contested tradition of "cultural studies audience research" in general (Nightingale, 1996) are important, but I would like to focus here on three notions of audiences from which theories of a global audience must draw upon (or depart from): the ideological, the resistive, and the elusive.

Ideological Audiences

The "ideological" notion of audiences may be located mainly in the early work associated with the British cultural studies tradition, beginning with

Hall's (1973/1993) theoretical outline spelled out in the encoding-decoding model. In this line of work, which is marked by a detailed concern for the core issues of meaning and power, audiences are seen as being "relatively autonomous" in their decoding practices of media (especially television) messages; a line of thinking following a larger conception of the social totality as overdetermined, both structural and cultural; and "without guarantees," as it were. In short, audiences are theorized (and suitable evidence also offered) as making different kinds of meanings from media texts, but a strong inclination seems implicit in this approach toward showing how these multiple meanings serve dominance rather than resistance.

The lasting contribution of this approach in audience studies, however, is the fact that the terrain of much of the location of audiencehood, such as everyday life, domesticity, and the all-important domain of commonsense within which people make sense of media have become important analytical areas. The study of audiences, hence, is used to demonstrate how apparently normal, natural, and commonsensical ways of thinking and feeling about mediated issues are in fact arbitrary, historical, constructed, and ideological, serving relations of power along class, gender, and other lines in specific historical contexts.

Resistive Audiences

Despite the emphasis on the relative autonomy of the media production and consumption processes in cultural studies, the study (and theorizing) of audiences has in some circles tended to a far more celebratory position that may be characterized as espousing a "resistive audience." Two lines of thinking about audiences in cultural studies—which do not necessarily privilege audience resistance over broader forms of hegemony—have been extended to argue in favor of resistive audiences: one, the notion that media texts are polysemic and incapable of foreclosing or imposing meaning upon audiences; two, a growing interest in popular and often "entertainment" forms of media (as opposed to what may be seen as "serious" media forms such as news and information programs) with their attendant "pleasures" for audiences.

In the context of the rapid globalization of cultural studies, and the ascendancy of global media corporations and globally distributed cultural forms since the 1980s, the rise to prominence of the notion of "resistive audiences" raises some troubling questions. On the one hand, there is a temptation to indeed take audience autonomy seriously in an international context, given the valid criticisms that have been made of traditional cultural imperialism theorists' implicit characterization of non-Western audiences as passive victims (Buell, 1994). On the other hand, it is impossible to ignore the growing domination, from the political-economy perspective, of a small number of transnational media corporations (Petras, 1993). Given these dilemmas, it would seem that in global media and cultural studies, the study of audiences would need to negotiate a course that acknowledges the relative autonomy of audiences without denying the dominant position of media institutions in a global context. Such a course has indeed been suggested by numerous critics of the resistive audience notion (Lewis, 1994; Morley, 1993), who have argued that polysemy and popular pleasure may extend the reach of hegemony rather than counter it.

Elusive Audiences

The most visible contemporary notion of audiences, however, seems to follow the resistive line rather than a more critical one and once again for the most contradictory of reasons. If the late 1970s and 1980s may be seen as the glory days for ideological and resistive notions of audiences, respectively, the 1990s have been dominated by a radical set of ideas that advocate the notion of "elusive audiences" by showing how "real" audiences can never be completely captured by the institutional discourses about them. Paralleling the broader rise of epistemological critiques of Western philosophy in the humanities and social sciences, a postmodernist argument about the unknowability of audiences has gained currency (Jensen, 1995). The contradictory (in a critical sense) nature of these developments is apparent in the fact that what began as a very valid critique of the institutional production of knowledge about audiences such as ratings research (Ang, 1990) has culminated in arguments that retreat from, if not explicitly abandon, the task of audience studies—precisely at a time when greater portions of the world's population are becoming global media audiences through technologies like satellite television.

In the context of global media studies, the rise of the notion of elusive audiences has meant a conflation of the terms "globalization" and "postmodernization" in important arguments such as those of Ang's (1996). Although Ang (1990) has also argued for the value of empirical audience studies in globalization, the same argument may be problematized by the conflation of the "global" and the "postmodern." The cautionary postmodernism evoked by Ang in critically highlighting the limits and political claims of modernity is certainly appropriate, but the move toward positing "unknowability" as a condition makes postmodernism guilty of the very certainties it seeks to critique.

Postcolonialism and Audience Studies

As postcolonialist scholars like R. Radhakrishnan (1994) have argued, postmodernism is in some ways merely another name for the imperialism perpetrated historically by a certain place (that it is no longer fashionable to call the "West") upon the rest of the world. This tension, in the context of audience studies, is seen by the fact that even a call to "openness" in theorization of audiences can work to close, and shut out, certain other theoretical positions (Juluri, 1998a). In other words, what authority can audience studies in, about, and from non-Western contexts claim globally when the Western academy, in the thrall of postmodernism, has decided there is nothing more to be said about audiences, particularly the *globality* of audiences?

The elusive audience of the global-postmodern envisioned within a certain moment in Western thought is clearly not empowering for the actual audiences (and others) caught up in the present-day experience of globalization. It may be true that the critical academic study of global media audiences is also engaged in the imagination of certain notions of audiences that are at best partial representations of the real world of global audiencehood. However, as Ganguly (1992) argues, these representations are fundamentally a matter of constituency, agency, and self-reflexivity. She points out that even if the critical-academic notion of the audience is a partial representation, it is still "a philosophically and politically motivated evocation of the real human beings in our inquiries" (p. 67) and is something worth exploring if anchored within a constituency and a project, whether it is postcolonialism, or postcolonialism and feminism, as in the case of Ganguly's argument.

It may also be true that the audience imagined by global media corporations in various nations will always be eluded by the complexity of the real world of audiences who will also make meanings in far more complex and multiple ways than that imagined or intended by media producers. This supposed elusiveness of real audiences does not, however, translate into a catch-all political resistance to global hegemony. Neither is such a resistance possible by researchers' writing strategies alone, as Natrajan and Parameswaran (1997) forcefully argue. Their suggestion, instead, is for a project that approaches "everyday life" as "struggle" rather than "resistance," with the goal of producing "alternative knowledge . . . [through]

Third World ethnographers writ[ing] about the everyday lives of Third World people with an awareness of the political need for claiming legitimacy as Third World scholars" (p. 53).

The present study may be seen as a contribution to such a project, and an attempt to construct a postcolonialist approach to global audiences, rather than a postmodern one as has been the case. Although the term "postcolonial" is sometimes misunderstood as a belief in the end of colonialism, or alternatively, scholarship devoted exclusively to historical issues from the era of "official" colonialism (Ashcroft, Griffiths, & Tiffin, 1998), it is more accurate and useful to describe this perspective as one that takes the historical experience of colonialism as central to the contemporary global condition. From such a perspective, this book draws its mandate and constituency. To continue a little further on questions of disciplinary locations in a multidisciplinary era, it is also useful to address the specificities of audience studies, and cultural studies, in general, as these are globalized. The networks, alliances, coalitions, and politics that have arisen between the tradition of British cultural studies and various anticolonialist cultural-political movements in various national contexts (Chen, 1998), and the place of the United States academy in relation to these, all have a bearing on the directions which audience studies could take. In addition, as numerous scholars have recently argued, the theorization of audiences in all directions (although mainly towards the resistive/elusive end) has diverted attention from the necessity for evidence, and empirical study (Gibson, 2000; Stromer-Galley & Schiappa, 1998). These tendencies have made, postmodernism notwithstanding, audience studies based on empirical research all the more valuable. From these traditions, this book draws its objects of study, and its methodology.

Reception and Impact under Globalization

Given the empirical and theoretical challenges presented to traditional debates about global media and audiences by the vast and rapid advent of satellite television in India, what sort of a research design could best address the question of impact? Would the relative strength of India in cultural production and the localization strategy of global media in India simply make the question of cultural imperialism irrelevant, or instead demand a closer rethinking of how cultural imperialism would work? A strict design for studying cultural imperialism would have to, in the words of Liebes and Katz (1993), first take up an American/Western program and then prove:

> (1) that there is a message incorporated in the program that is designed to profit American interests overseas (2) that the message is decoded by the receiver in the way it was encoded by the sender, and (3) that it is accepted uncritically by the viewers and allowed to seep into their culture. (p. 4)

While this sketches out a logical framework for assessing the reception of global media and testing the hypothesis of cultural imperialism, the historical realities of media globalization in India as well as the theoretical contributions of audience studies make such assumptions untenable. Thus, in the case of music television in India, American programs or videos may not constitute a significant portion of programming, these programs may not necessarily serve American interests as much as those of multinational media companies (including their Indian partners), these messages may be decoded differently from the way they were encoded (presuming that encoding and intentionality are easily identifiable), and they may not be accepted uncritically. However, these criticisms should not be taken to mean that there is no justification for claiming, studying, or critiquing cultural imperialism.

To invoke John Tomlinson (1991), the media imperialism thesis may not so much be wrong, as "wrongly formulated" (p. 58). Tomlinson's position is that while there is no denying cultural imperialism given the imperialistic nature of the global system of capitalist modernity, it is impossible to find empirical evidence of cultural imperialism through audience studies. Such studies, according to Tomlinson, only end up confirming that the audience is a little more active than originally thought to be and do little else. On this note, Tomlinson's criticisms are instructive, especially since it is difficult to make judgments on the basis of single texts and their reception. Instead, one useful way to approach issues of meaning and audience activity would be in terms of flows[3] and themes, as these may point out what may be most socially and culturally relevant at any given time. Specific texts chosen to represent these themes must be seen not so much as individual texts, but as samples of these themes instead. In other words, the significance of studying specific texts lies in the fact that, as Jensen (1995) says, "whatever impact one text can be said to have is . . . reinforced by intertextuality" (p. 120). Thus, if the meanings that audience members make of certain texts can be assessed within the broader historical context as indicating some kind of impact, it follows that the broader intertextuality of television flows may be having a profound impact at the larger social level as well. While music television programs in India have produced a wide range of genres and conventions, I focus on one genre in particular in this study—the music countdown show.

At the time of this study, there were at least 32 music countdown shows available on a variety of channels—although most of these shows featured the same songs, namely, Indian movie hits (see Appendix B). While Channel V and MTV had the most number of countdowns, including a metachart on Channel V featuring the "number one" songs from all its other charts, other nonmusic television channels presented music countdowns at the intersection of other genres: sitcoms (Doordarshan's *All the Best*), political satire in the form of "mock shows," or a spoof of talk shows (Gemini's *Santoor Top Ten*), quiz shows in which participants try to guess what song appears next on the chart (Home TV's *Hit Hit Hurray*), and travel shows featuring tourist spots in India and abroad (EL TV's *Superhit Hungama*). The countdown format has also been extended beyond music, and there are various programs that present "top tens" and "top fives" of other aspects of popular culture such as films and film stars' ratings (on the informal basis of their films' success). On a related note, bestseller lists (for music, books, and video circulation) have become more widespread in newspapers and magazines as well in recent years.

As a widespread TV genre, the countdown is fairly new to Indian audiences. Although film song-based programming has been one of Doordarshan's most popular genres since the 1970s—and still is—through programs like *Chitrahar* (Hindi) and its regional language versions like *Chitralahari* (Telugu) and *Oliyum Oliyum* (Tamil), these programs did not use the countdown format. Thus, until the time of the satellite television boom, film songs appeared on television with little emphasis on presentation by way of charts, fillers, graphics, or VJs. In addition, programs like *Chitrahar* seldom played current hits. Western pop music also occasionally appeared on Doordarshan, but once again, did not use the countdown format.[4]

The countdown boom of the 1990s may be seen in some ways as having come from outside India, considering the fact that MTV was one of the first channels to have popularized the format. In addition, the countdowns presently available on satellite television may also be classified on the basis of their music as being global (on the basis of the worldwide dissemination of Western music on shows like *Billboard*), continental (programs like *Asian Top 20*), national (*Indian Top 10*, as well as Channel V's other national countdowns for Thailand, Korea, Japan, and the Philippines), and regional (especially in South Indian languages).

The relationship between the proliferation of countdowns and the experience of globalization for audiences may be appreciated by acknowledging that the characterization of countdowns as a genre is as much a theoretical move as a description of an empirical reality. As Jane Feuer

(1992) points out, television genres are not necessarily coherent categories that may be simply identified exclusively on the basis of textual or "aesthetic" considerations, but represent, in specific historical contexts, "a consensus between the industry, *TV Guide*, and the viewing audience" (p. 146). The music countdown may thus be seen as a way in which the political economy of music television in India has enabled certain discourses of popularity and representation to emerge as exemplified in the top ten chart. While the sheer scale of availability of music countdowns at these levels may justify its characterization as a "global" genre, studying its emergence in the context of globalization within a specific national context calls for a more nuanced understanding. While it may be possible to argue that the "form" of the genre may be transnational while its "content" is often national or subnational, as in the case of India, the form/content distinction is only a starting point for analysis. On the other hand, if countdowns were classified on the basis of their music, that would imply that only Western music-based countdowns are "global," given their worldwide reach—and stop short with programs like Channel V's *Indian Top Ten*, which play Indian and Western pop music. In addition, the equation of "Western" and "global," the empirical truth of the global domination of Western media production notwithstanding, would also imply that the study of globalization would have to be restricted to the reception of Western programming in various countries—although, as in the case of India, Western programs do not necessarily get the highest ratings.

Instead, globalization is perhaps better understood by examining the rise of a particular genre as a whole within a certain historical context. In other words, rather than assume that TV viewers in India switch from being global, national, and regional viewers with each push of the remote control, it is more useful to situate the rise of the countdown genre itself in the wider social and cultural forces that may be said to characterize globalization, as well as its national inflection in India in the name of liberalization. A genre may thus be seen, in the words of Jesus Martin-Barbero (1993), as "constituting a 'world'" in specific contexts, not simply through its aesthetic or taxonomic elements, but by the functioning of its "architecture," which in turn illustrates how the system of genres in different countries serves to articulate these countries into the "transnational system" (p. 224).

Countdowns in India may thus be seen as an example of how audiences negotiate, at the levels of daily life, family relations and everyday temporalities, the broader network of capitalist production, relations, and temporalities at the national and transnational levels. By the sheer fact of their rather sudden appearance in the early 1990s and their proliferation, countdowns may thus be taken as an important and representative example of a television genre that would unlock some of the ways in which the local, the national, and the global have begun to interact since liberalization in India. These interactions may be seen not only in terms of broader social experiences of spatialities, temporalities, and family ties and relationships, but also in terms of the intelligibilities that are constituted in the light of these changing social experiences around the genre on the basis of access to cultural competence.

Research Design

While certain genre conventions and themes stand out as postglobalization features in Indian music television, it is useful to acknowledge that not all aspects have the same relevance, value, or even intelligibility for viewers. Foregrounding audience readings in the construction of the preferred meaning of texts is not only theoretically useful (Lewis, 1983), but also practically helpful given the fact that the vast quantitative increase in television "flows" (Jensen, 1995) in India consists not only of increased numbers of programs but also of an increased semiotic density in specific parts of the program. For example, even a single frame from a music countdown show would contain a great deal of information: the overall multiscreen layout, consisting of the show's distinctive background and various graphics including the name of the show. Then, the song or video (which may itself be broken into further frames) is presented, along with pervasive indicators of the song's ranking on the charts, including numbers, graphs, smiling/neutral/sad faces bobbing up and down ladders, and such. Meanwhile, the soundtrack could consist of "signature" phrases and tunes before and after the song, filler music, and in general a great deal of noise.

Viewing Segments

Such microscopic attention may not be methodologically feasible, but needs to be noted all the same, as these are all textual features that are not only pervasive, but also distinctive to a large extent of contemporary television in India—even as these may have been naturalized and routinized by viewers. However, for the purpose of facilitating discussion in a group interview format, four representative segments were selected in this study. The first segment selected for the interviews consisted of excerpts from the title sequences of three countdown shows. All the title sequences contained graphics pertaining to numbers, and while that of *Indian Top Ten* and *Santoor Top Ten* featured instrumental theme music, *Superhit Muqabla* featured a song with lyrics in Hindi exhorting viewers to watch the weekly competition between songs for the number one spot. The second segment represented a portion from the program, including a VJ's presentation, two songs, and the graphics and fillers in between. Three different clips were used for different viewing groups: from *Indian Top Ten* for viewers familiar with international pop, from *Santoor Top Ten* for exclusively Telugu viewers, and from *Superhit Muqabla* for viewers who found Hindi film music most familiar. This segment was aimed at opening up a general discussion about music, taste, the role of VJs, and the visual aspects of the songs.

The third segment, which was shown to all groups, was Alisha Chinai's *Made in India* video, and was used to stimulate discussion about national identity and globalization in the context of music television. Although the song was not current on any of the countdowns (except as flashback fare), it was used because of viewer familiarity with it and its historic importance as one of Indian pop's first videos as well as its theme about competition between Indians and other nationals in a fairy tale romantic setting. The final viewing segment consisted of an excerpt from "public" shows. For most of the interviews, a segment from *Public Demand* was used; in the first part of the clip, the VJ asks people on a street "what is the best way to reach God," and gets a range of responses, including "Concorde, because God believes in modernization," and in the second part of the clip, a group of *dhaba* (tea-stall) workers are shown cooking and eating and saying "Public Demand" as the song number appears. For the remaining interviews, which consisted of people who watched Telugu channels more or less exclusively, a segment from ETV's *Hrudayanjali* (a "public" show with current film hits but not a countdown) showing the VJ interviewing students in a girls' high school in a small town was used.

Interview Questions

Interview questions were framed around these four viewing segments, beginning with open-ended questions about how many countdowns participants could name and which ones they watched. In order to get a sense of how viewers distinguished the countdown genre, they were asked to compare the new countdown shows with what used to be the most popular program featuring film songs in the past, *Chitrahar* on Doordarshan (and its regional versions). Viewers were also asked to describe what they thought the countdowns' title clips were trying to say. Questions after the second clip began with the specific songs they had just watched and moved on to their tastes in music in general. This part of the interview was aimed at covering a broad range of issues including the family context of viewing. Questions about the *Made in India* video were more specific, and aimed at getting a sense of how viewers made sense of being "Indian" in terms of character and values in relation to the rest of the world. The public segment was aimed to get viewer responses to the genre in general, and questions were directed to their broad like/dislike for these shows rather than what participants in the specific segments said or did. Viewers were also asked to select who among the people interviewed was a better example of the public (the people who spoke or the people who merely appeared as fillers). Finally, two broad questions were used to get a sense of the larger context of satellite television in present-day India. Viewers were asked to describe what they thought had changed in their lives and in society since the beginning of satellite television, and what the term "globalization" suggested to them.

The Participants

In principle, the universe for participants in this study consisted of "music television viewers," which is by no means an exclusive category since no channels are watched exclusively in India (Sahai, 1997). At the same time, the ubiquity of music-related programming implies that large numbers of viewers are indeed music television viewers as well. Participants were recruited with the following criteria: they had to be familiar with music programs on television and willing to talk about them. One problem with access was that a number of people who declined to participate clearly watched many of these programs, but felt they did not "know enough" to participate. This tendency appeared in the early stages of some of the interviews as well, where some participants seemed hesitant, as if looking for the "correct" answer. On the whole, however, participants seemed comfortable and willing to talk, and their having been invited by key informants in familiar peer groups also contributed to the positive environment.

Nine group interviews were conducted, consisting of 42 participants, most of whom may be described as middle to upper class in terms of socioeconomic privilege, and ranging in age from their mid-teens to early 30s—from high school to university levels (most of them were students or young professionals). The main exception to this was one group that consisted exclusively of older domestic workers and their elementary-school level children, and a few other working-class participants who joined some of the other groups. The members of this group, as well as some other members, also did not have cable/satellite connections (see Appendix A). The first group consisted of four first-year intermediate (grade 11) science students from a women's junior college. Two of them seemed to have greater familiarity with international pop music and culture than the others, who were mainly viewers of Hindi language programming. The second interview was very animated and consisted of a group of third-year commerce students from a prestigious women's college, and a former student who was at that time working as a freelance writer. Every single member of this group had a lot of things to say (often at the same time, making for some difficult transcribing), and this group displayed the greatest knowledge/recall of shows and facts. The high interest level with which they participated became evident early in the interview, when they sang along and yelled responses to the screening clips. All the members of this group also seemed well ensconced in the pop idiom of MTV and Channel V.

Three subsequent interviews took place at the University of Hyderabad's Golden Threshold campus (an old and idyllic bungalow in the heart of Hyderabad that used to be the residence of nationalist poet Sarojini Naidu). The first of these groups consisted of three final-year college students who had been invited by one of the Mass Communication students at the University who had offered to help me. They were broadly knowledgeable about many of the shows and very articulate, but were not necessarily fans of MTV/Channel V. The second group consisted of graduate students in the dance program. They were most comfortable with Telugu films programs but were also critical of obscenity in Indian film culture. The third group consisted of graduate students in the art program and had a slightly wider range in terms of age, class, and regional background than the other groups. They were interested in television for the information aspect, which was very important to them, and addressed countdowns as something they enjoyed, but did not get too absorbed in (two members indicated that they were fans of Indian and Western classical music and did not particularly like film and pop music).

Two group interviews took place at the joint family residence of a friend. The first of these groups consisted of high-school students who seemed to occupy a comfortable space in Hindi/Indian pop music culture, while also being familiar with Channel V/MTV and international music. The second group consisted of a domestic worker who worked in their house, her neighbor, and their children (in middle and primary school).

This group was quite different from the others, and not at all involved with some of the discourses about music and television that had appeared in the other interviews. However, the two adults in this group spoke eloquently, especially toward the end of the interviews, about their lives, work, television, music, and their hopes for their children (all of whom, they were proud to say, went to school).

The last two interviews took place in the apartment of another friend who did not participate but organized all the members and hospitality as well. The first of these groups consisted of his university colleagues who were working on a wildlife research project: two postdoctoral scholars, a wildlife officer, and their project assistant. This was the group I could relate to most closely, given age and educational similarities, and found a great deal of information and opportunity for discussion. One member of this group was passionate about music, and his interests spanned a wide range, while others were fairly well informed about Hindi and/or Telugu film music. The second group consisted of neighbors and visitors; a very articulate high-school student, an undergraduate science student, another member of the wildlife research project (who had walked in late), and two middle-aged professionals, one of whom worked in the Middle East. The discussion in this group came for the most part from the younger members. The older participants mentioned old film songs they liked frequently but did not connect with the countdown-related questions at all.

Location and Representativeness

The majority of the participants are fairly representative of the universe of cable/satellite viewers in India, and particularly, in terms of class and age, of the main audience for the international music television channels. In addition, they are also more representative of an urban rather than a rural audience, although at least one participant hailed from a rural background and was living in the university hostel. While the study's setting in Hyderabad may provide an example of any Indian urban context, the city's distinctiveness is also relevant. Hyderabad is the fifth largest city in India, with a population of about five million, and has recently embarked towards what urban planners called "megacity" status (Iyengar, 1994). As the capital of Andhra Pradesh, one of the four large South Indian states and the fifth largest state in the country, Hyderabad is in some ways a South Indian metropolis but also quite hybrid in terms of religion, language, and culture. Finally, in the context of liberalization, Hyderabad provides an interesting example. On the one hand, it is being promoted as an industrial and information-technology center while at the same time it is not necessarily as important a market for global brands as Mumbai or Bangalore.[5] At the same time, Hyderabad is a useful site, as it is one of the few cities where English, Hindi, and regional language channels are all widely watched, and the Telugu film industry is one of the three largest ones in India (besides Hindi and Tamil).

Analysis

Following Lunt and Livingstone (1996), a systematic qualitative approach was employed in analyzing the interview data. The interviews were transcribed and manually coded. While the transcription process and early reviews of the interviews enabled the formulation of some broad reactions to key features of the interviews—including a "feel" for what was happening—the process of systematic coding allowed for a more precise estimation of what facts seemed most salient. The contents of the interviews were exhaustively coded and counted for frequencies of responses. There was a clear indication on the basis of the frequencies of the importance of some items in the interviews. For instance, there were ten responses in the category "I pay attention to the ranking of songs on countdown shows," as opposed to only one response in the category "the ranking of songs is not important to me." Such findings were taken as evidence of patterns that may be fairly widespread across the population of young urban middle-class television viewers in India and specific excerpts pertaining to these points were emphasized for further analysis.

At this point, it is also useful to acknowledge that no interview can exhaustively represent the experience of reception. Reception studies are reliant on participants' ability and willingness to verbalize their experience, and while this may be a limitation, it does not necessarily diminish the usefulness of such research. Evidence of their reception experience may be constituted as much by what is not said. As Lewis (1991) points out, the "silences" in interviews are important to analysis as well because they indicate the limits of intelligibility of certain discourses; in other words, what is "unspeakable" in the sense of being outside the scope of imagination and knowledge for participants.

Finally, it must be noted that while the question of determination is central to any analysis, what participants say does not necessarily imply that it is only their class or any other single determinant speaking through them. Instead, the contents of their speech (and their silences) are better appreciated in terms of how they are enabled and constrained by their access to certain kinds of cultural competencies, which in turn rests on their access to material privileges in general. The use of terms like "middle class" and "working class" is used in this study to emphasize differences in such access—because these differences are important—but not to reduce participants to their class positions defined by occupation and/or income. In addition, given the complexity of the issue of class in general, and especially its intersections with caste, religion, and other variables in the Indian context, the findings of this study should be seen not so much as a class-based comparison of reception, but instead as an attempt to situate reception in a social and historic context that is marked by profound differences in access to privilege at the local, national, and global levels.

Becoming Global

One objective of this study is to advance, following Stuart Hall (1997), an understanding of globality as something more than the "lowest common denominator." I do not invoke the "global audience" in this book to imply that my findings and arguments represent young MTV viewers all around the world, but do so as an investment in the possibility that something much larger, deeper, and more important that we could call the "global condition" is indeed represented. My conclusions in this book are an attempt to recognize such a possibility in what I believe is the main thrust in audience investments and interpretations in the broad meaning of music television: the feeling of being *represented*. At its core, this is indeed a feeling, an immersion in a subjective experience that is highly valued, desired, and essentially larger than the individual self. The main parameters of this experience are what one television producer calls "emotions" and "relationships" (quoted in Unnikrishnan, 2002). However, the framing of this experience within the new discursive terms entailed by postglobalization music television lends new dimensions to the notion of being represented. Audiences claim a sense of representation also in the modern, imagined, self-relativizing terms of being represented as the public and the nation in a global context.

The desires underlying these readings seem commendable. Participants claim a sense of belonging with each other across class lines in the notion of the "public" and exemplify the nature of their sense of belonging in the notion of the "nation" through an evocation of Indians as selfless mothers, fathers, children, siblings, and friends—an evocation many of them believe or hope would be acknowledged by the West. However,

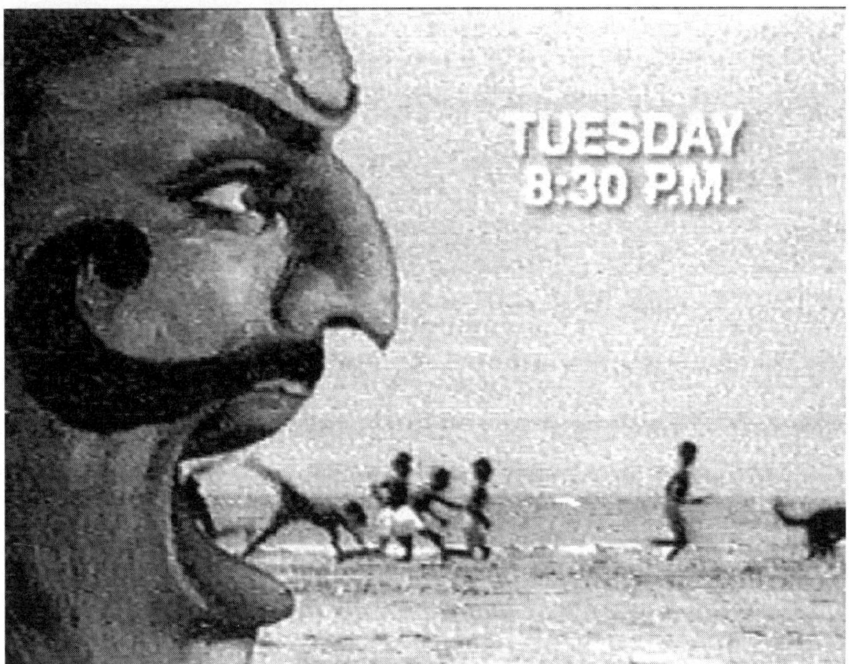

FIGURE 2 Exoticizing the everyday. A promo for Channel V's program Simply South shows film poster cut-outs and children on a beach in a surreal manner.

the sense of belonging that participants find in music television raises a number of troubling questions, given the specific images and discourses in which they are beginning to see themselves as being represented. The images of the "public" are to a large extent based on a new Channel V- and MTV-driven fad of exoticizing and ridiculing working-class people in promos and videos. The images of the "nation" in which participants find their Indian *dil* ("heart") are plainly orientalistic—elephants, soothsayers, princes, and so on.

My contention is that these examples are part of a profound change in commonsensical, everyday notions about a number of areas of life that range from the imagined (such as the national and the global) to the immediate and the intense (such as the family and interpersonal relationships), and that these notions serve to normalize the reordering of social relations under the deeply political project that is globalization. In terms of the role of media in particular in this process, however, I advance a critique not so much of audience gullibility or victimization (or of an all-encompassing economic determination by media corporations), but of a failure of imagination in cultural self-representation (despite the tremendous expression of creative talent in Indian television since liberalization). To call this a failure is not to point the blame at media producers alone—for the representations they may be criticized for are as much signs of the new global condition (and an old historical one) as they are creations of their individual imagination—but to appreciate and theorize collectively the impact of satellite television in India in the context of globalization. This impact, as I argue, is not so much a model of injection of foreign values or ideologies but instead one of appropriation—of all that has been cherished, valued, worth living for—toward the powerful forces of contemporary politics.

In the context of contemporary cultural politics in India, the findings of this study explore such issues of power along two main lines: the changes in the perception of class relations entailed in the project of liberalization, and the emerging perceptions of national identity in a global context entailed in the project of globalization. Liberalization and globalization are clearly overlapping phenomena and may be situated in some discourses as being identical, or a part of the other. In this study, however, the two terms are used somewhat differently in order to map different but related lines of thinking among the Indian middle class in relation to certain music television discourses. Both terms, however, are used in this study toward a shared goal: the critique of relations of power, privilege, and accountability, particularly in terms of class and nation.

The politics of meaning and definition that are explored in this study are best understood, I believe, by naming as such an emerging sense of a "global India"—particularly its emergence as a generationally inflected locus of identification. Recent discussion of media and cultural politics in India has focused on the rise of religious revivalism (Rajagopal, 2000). It is my contention, however, that this phenomenon is best put in perspective by addressing the broader politics of globality in Indian everyday life—in other words, how a sense of the world and one's place in it emerges in relation to media, a sense that may be characterized as "Global India." Global India may be understood as an ideal for which many Indians who are implicated in becoming global audiences are longing for. This phenomenon has domestic implications, in the form of perceptions of liberalization as freedom from government control, as seen in audience readings of the "public." More explicitly, this phenomenon presents a shiny new nationalism that is global in its outlook and imagination and youth-oriented in its appeal, but derives its energy from the ties and emotions of family relations. Global India is, however, a hegemonic formation, and gains its consent at the interface of an imperial globality and another perhaps undefined, globality.

A critical understanding of this phenomenon calls for a variety of approaches and methodologies. As such, this book deploys insights and perspectives drawn from numerous intellectual traditions ranging from political economy to postcolonial theory. In Chapter 1, I address the commercial context of music television in India, and show how a particular articulation of the television, film, and music industries under the expediencies of economic liberalization have led to the proliferation of music television channels and programs. In Chapter 2, I outline the main features of the reception of music television and argue that the relative autonomy of viewing music television in comparison to listening to music is central to an appreciation of the normalization of various music television conventions in reception practices. Chapter 3 takes on the music countdown genre in depth, and shows how participants' reading of this genre indicates an investment in an egalitarian sense of the "public" that is unfortunately belied by the real context of class relations in Indian everyday life under economic liberalization. In Chapter 4, I critique a similar investment made by participants in the idea of the nation in a global context, focusing on the meanings made by them of the music video of "Made in India" and situating these in the broader discourses of nation and world that have proliferated in Indian media. Finally, in Chapter 5, I examine from a postcolonialist perspective the epistemic differences in the reception of music television as a whole and argue that a recognition of an alternative globality based on "emotions" and "relationships" is necessary if globalization is indeed to become "the next historical project" (Hall, 1997) that we are not merely swept up in but also in some limited ways "knowingly" embarking upon.

CHAPTER 1

THE COMMERCIAL CONTEXT OF MUSIC TELEVISION IN INDIA

MTV . . . [was] . . . an international channel with international music . . . ramming Western music down everyone's throats.
—Channel V GM Don Atyeo (quoted in Hussain, 1997)

[Channel] V is in the territory of international music which young Indians certainly don't love.
—MTV India GM Sunil Lulla (quoted in "It's open war," 1997)

Channel V and MTV . . . are trying to be Indian (but) their look is still very Western.
—Music Asia GM Madhavi Mutatkar (quoted in "Music Asia . . . ," 1997)

The entry of global media into satellite television operations in India has not taken the form of a deluge of Western programming. Despite this seeming genuflection of global capital to national culture, the emergence of music television in India is underscored by a profound change in the mandate originally envisioned for television as a part of the project of postcolonial nationhood. If the Doordarshan audience was imagined as consisting of citizen viewers (in need of modernization and some firm instruction on the merits of the ruling party), the post-liberalization television audience is being imagined as consisting of five *paise*[1] consumers.

Although I would not ascribe all that I examine in this book to the generative powers of the five-paise coin, its evocative significance in the "first instance" (Hall, 1986) must be noted, particularly in the context of the political economy and cultural studies debates. While I do not wish to overstate the importance of these debates, it would be useful to acknowledge that the goals of political economy serve to strengthen the critical edge of cultural studies, while cultural studies in turn simply brings political economy to life by understanding media and audiences (among other things) not necessarily as sites of resistance, but as sites of struggle (Garnham, 1995; Grossberg, 1995). My aim in this chapter is to describe how—and with what social and political costs—the construction of the music television audience in India has come about in and through the economic logics of media globalization.

Liberalization and Television

In his study of telecommunications policy in India, Stephen McDowell (1997) makes the useful distinction that economic liberalization needs to be understood not merely as a "withdrawal of state intervention from economic production and exchange" but instead as a move toward "greater use of market mechanisms to guide social, economic and political aspects of collective life" (p. 38). The Indian state had been a facilitator of marketization in many ways even before the present phase of liberalization was inaugurated in 1991 (Kurien, 1994). A key issue, and one with direct relation to television in both phases of liberalization, however, is that of national economic sovereignty in a global context. It would seem, following Kurien, that the liberalization of the 1980s under the Congress Party did not have the kind of external compulsions shaping its direction the way that liberalization in the 1990s did, and was (mis)directed toward the consumer sector mainly because of the nexus of domestic politics and business. An important outcome of this phase, however, was the massive growth of consumer electronics in India, and the beginning of the commercialization of Doordarshan.

In a manner of speaking, the Indian television audience was thus largely built during the 1980s, and was simply there for the taking by global media corporations (and their Indian collaborators) when the next wave of liberalization came around. This time, however, as Kurien argues, India had little choice but to accept the long-term "structural adjustment" diktats of the World Bank in the face of growing foreign and domestic economic pressures. Even as these policies began the transformation of India into a captive market in the global economy, Hong Kong-based Star TV[2] began beaming into Indian homes in 1991.

The response to the Star TV network in India was incredibly energetic, and quite symptomatic of the nature of post-liberalization enterprise and (non)regulation. Access to Star TV was provided by enterprising neighborhood cable operators who rapidly wired up subscribers to satellite dishes, seizing a moment of confused inaction on the part of the government. As McDowell (1997) writes, "The cable television distribution industry jumped from being almost nonexistent to achieving extensive coverage in urban areas in two to three years time in the early 1990s" (p. 215). The growth of cable providers in India was essentially an unregulated activity, built by "upstart business ventures" (p. 215) and it is largely local and cut-throat at times.[3]

The response of the Indian government to satellite television was somewhat mixed. The absence of social vision or political will (except for the expediencies of liberalization) facilitated the early proliferation of satellite television and cable. Although some degree of state regulation has been imposed more recently with the passing of the Cable Networks Regulation Act in 1995, the more far-reaching Broadcasting Bill[4] continues to be debated. The state's great strength in television was found, however, not so much in its regulatory powers, but in its control of Doordarshan. Doordarshan's monopoly status as a terrestrial broadcaster gave it a wide and exclusive reach that satellite channels could hardly emulate. At the same time, Doordarshan faced the challenge not only of having to adjust to decreased state funding, but of having to be competitive in an intense multichannel television environment.

This became especially necessary with the rise of Zee TV in October 1992. Zee emerged as the first private Indian language television channel and with its relentless entertainment agenda cut into portions of Doordarshan's hitherto untouched mass national audience. Zee became an instant success with the emerging Indian middle class, as well as viewers in the Middle East long familiar with Indian cinema. Shah (1997) points out that as many as 85,000 letters arrived each day from across West and South Asia, full of praise for its programs. Alarmed by the growing popularity of Zee, and the impending loss of advertising revenues, Doordarshan launched its own counteroffensive, with successful and, on occasion, ludicrous effects.

Even as proposed programming guidelines for Doordarshan's new channels were being debated, it went ahead and launched the Metro Channel, relying largely on Indian film-based programming. With the success of the Metro Channel, and the launch of numerous satellite channels featuring regional language programming, Doordarshan increased its presence, but continued to face the problem of finding programming. Its initial announcement about allotting programs to independent producers on a first-come first-served basis, which was subsequently legally challenged in 1993, had the preposterous effect of having two lines of prospective producers form outside its office in New Delhi for days, each claiming to be the "correct one" (Shah, 1997, p. 124).

However, the absence of coherence did not deter the battle for audiences that began to unfold between Doordarshan and Zee. In programming terms, this basically came down to a battle of film music countdowns. Doordarshan's Sunday evening countdown *Superhit Muqabla* became a massive hit. At the same time, Zee came up with its own countdown called *Phillips Top Ten*, which went on to gather some of the highest viewership ratings for satellite television programs (Ninan, 1995). Both countdowns featured the latest Hindi film songs, and differed mainly in terms of what they featured between the songs, experimenting with a variety of formats over the years. However, these shows established film music-based shows as the backbone of postliberalization television programming in India, and countdowns in particular as a prolific genre.

Music Television and Mass Audiences

Music-based programs have since come to constitute the basis of mass audience programming. Doordarshan's film music countdowns, *Superhit Muqabla*, *All the Best*, and *Ek Se Badkar Ek*, as well as longer running programs like *Chitrahar* (and its regional language variants), became high ratings earners. Among satellite television programs, Zee's *Philips Top Ten*, and the film music-based game show *Antakshari* gained the highest ratings. The regional language satellite channels that began operations in the mid-1990s also turned to film music-based programs. For instance, Philips sponsored a satirical countdown called *Super 10* in Tamil on Sun TV. A similar format, featuring a combination of a film music countdown with political satire, was used by *Santoor Top Ten* on Gemini TV, a Telugu satellite channel that was acquired by the Sun TV group in 1997.

Film music-based programs have also been at the forefront of programming in the numerous channels aimed at national mass audiences that had begun broadcasting by the late 1990s. Although Doordarshan remains at the forefront of this category by virtue of its terrestrial monopoly, Zee TV, as the leading satellite channel, began to face competition from Sony Entertainment Television (SET) and Home TV, as well as Star Plus, the latter announcing its own Indianization plans in 1996. Initially, Star Plus attempted an easy route to mass audiences by simply dubbing English programs into Hindi. The incongruity of shows like *The Simpsons* in Hindi, however, supposedly put off its upper-class English-speaking viewers. Since then, Star Plus continued to focus on Hindi programming (Sehgal, 1997). For instance, in the summer of 1997, Star Plus premiered its own Hindi film music countdown, *Oo La La*, featuring Hindi film star

Neelam as "Couch Potato," a solitary viewer who watches songs and spoofs of Star Plus programs in between.

The proliferation of music-based programs across national and regional channels aiming to reach large audiences has come about not only because of their perceived commercial success in a competitive environment, but also because of the relatively low costs involved in producing them. Although dubbing Western programs and Indian productions into various other languages is the cheapest production route available (Rs. 20,000, or $500 per half-hour episode in comparison to up to Rs. 500,000, or $12,000 for an original production), film music-based programming has emerged as a viable alternative.

For countdowns in particular, production costs are often lower than those for soap operas or sitcoms. Film clips are often provided at no cost by film producers, as this provides publicity for the film.[5] Similarly, music videos are provided at no cost by the music companies. While the specific costs of production may vary depending on fillers used between songs in the countdown, for the most part all that is required is a single presenter and a single camera. In addition, countdown producers sometimes tape as many as half a dozen episodes in a single session, and use this footage to assemble specific episodes later.

The low production costs of countdowns are especially attractive for producers, since many of them are somewhat more vulnerable to financial pressures than advertisers and TV networks. While some channels have their own in-house production units (or purchase cheaper programming from other channels), independent producers are often required to take their own risks. For instance, if an independent producer wished to produce a Hindi sitcom for Doordarshan, this process would entail an initial investment of at least Rs. 300,000 (about $8,000) for the pilot episode out of which the main actors' fees, especially if these are famous TV stars, would form as much as one-sixth (Vesuna, 1995). Once the pilot is approved, the channel allots the producer dates and timeslots, as well as a certain amount of Free Commercial Time (FCT), which may be about 90 seconds as in the case of Doordarshan. The producer then sells this time to advertisers either directly or through a marketing agency. In the case of Doordarshan, however, producers' investment does not end with production, as they are often asked to deposit a Minimum Bank Guarantee of as much as Rs. 2,500,000 ($600,000) with the channel in case it is unable to get sufficient advertising. Other channels may not impose this risk on producers, and instead offer a flat rate per episode once a program is commissioned.

Independent producers often sell their programs to television marketing agencies such as Multichannel, which in turn sell advertising time to advertisers. Advertising agencies have formed their own opinions about commercial viability, which also tend to favor tested formulae like the countdown show. As one advertising executive says, "chat-shows are not very viable, a sitcom is good, a good soap is very good, and a film or film-based programmes are favourites" (quoted in Vesuna, 1995). Advertisers' support for countdowns may also be located in some of the specificities of emerging business practices in tune with a commercial system, including the new and contentious area of television ratings research,[6] as well as channel and program branding.[7] Countdowns provide the viewership figures upon which advertisers increasingly depend, and also greater visibility and association for sponsoring brands. Moreover, in the face of a relative setback in advertising growth during the mid-1990s that was attributed in part to low multinational product sales in the Indian market,[8] advertising priorities tended toward the established programs and genres once again.

The proliferation of music-based programs in general and countdowns in particular on mass audience-oriented channels is also attributed by media planners to a perception that "cloning" is a safe bet in the absence of sophisticated audience "profiling" techniques (Sharon & Hussain, 1997). Music television programs have thus emerged as one of the main choices for advertisers and media planners dealing with an attractively large but somewhat uncertain and undifferentiated mass audience. Music television channels, however, offer the possibility of carving out a youth market over the long run. Despite the present constraints on programming imposed by the demands of mass and niche marketing, the emergence of MTV and Channel V in particular may be appreciated in this context.

Music Television and the Youth Audience

While Doordarshan and Zee opened up the possibilities of music-based programming as a feasible strategy for reaching a mass audience, music television channels have been competitive in the Indian market as well. MTV, which had been one of the few channels originally featured on the Star TV platform, mostly played Western and East Asian pop music videos at that time, but was already quite popular for its VJs and its Indian countdown, *Oye MTV,* by the time it went off the Star TV platform in 1994. MTV did not find its way back into Indian households for a few years, but some of its VJs and programs moved to a new music television network on the Star TV platform, namely, Channel V.

Since its inception in the summer of 1994, Channel V quickly became synonymous with music television and youth culture in India. It followed Zee's "Indianization" lead with gusto and creativity, inaugurating a channel that would be simultaneously global and Indian. Channel V initially broadcast as a pan-Asian service, but then switched to a double-beam, broadcasting in Mandarin in one, and in Hindi and English in the other. Its reinvention as an Indian music television channel was enabled by its support for Indian pop music and its steady reliance on Indian film music (including the countdown *BPL Oye*). However, it was Channel V's idiosyncratic and self-consciously "Indian" promos (most notably, the South Indian movie cowboy character Quick Gun Murugan), and its self-conscious use of Indian-English ("V are like this only") that best established its presence among young audiences.

The guiding principle for Channel V was to reportedly "localize or bust," and while it did so extensively, it also faced a problem that few other satellite channels in India until that point had; namely, that of sustaining itself as a niche channel (Hussain, 1997). Channel V faced distribution problems because most television households in India are single-set ones. In addition, most TV sets are not fully cable ready (cannot carry more than a dozen channels), making the cultivation of niche audiences difficult. In addition, cable operators also had to be convinced to include Channel V in their main lineup. Another problem was that advertisers were somewhat skeptical, given the fact that the mass audience remained a more feasible target for them. The value of a 24-hour music channel did not seem apparent given the dominance of music-based programming on other channels.

Channel V's response to these constraints emerged in its particular vision of itself as a brand. It positioned itself as a channel for the "Young and Young at heart," a "family channel in audience demographics and a youth channel in attitude" (Hussain, 1997, p. 8). In terms of programming, this implied that Indian film music would play an important role, but would be presented in a format that would be appealing enough to young viewers. As Channel V's Jules Fuller put it, "We took the gamble of telling the kids, 'Look at film music; it's really cool'" (quoted in Hussain, 1997, p. 8).

Channel V's positioning pioneered a nascent form of youth culture centered around television, music, and the urban middle-class audience. Coupled with the strategy of localization, the youth culture of Channel V also expressed itself as a stylish nationalism. The strategies of youth marketing and localization were related to a rather well-thought-out perception among media planners that the emergent generation in India would have very different investments in national identity than earlier generations. For the young, it was believed, national identity would be defined largely through consumption—as opposed to their parents, whose own youth had been tempered by "Nehruvian austerity." Marketing executives believed, however, that the "midnight's children" generation of parents were actually encouraging consumerism among their children, allegedly in order to vicariously compensate for what they had missed (Bijapurkar, 1998). This perception may also be situated in relation to an Asia-wide marketing study of young people that showed a phenomenon called "rebelling in" (to the middle class) rather than "rebelling out" (against parents) by the young (McCaughan, 1998). For example, young people in India voted for Bill Gates as the man they would most like to emulate.

Given these peculiar configurations of class, mobility, and generationality in the 1990s, the youth audience that music television and advertisers sought came to be approached in the most ingenious of ways. Channel V not only had to be "cool" enough for young viewers, but also not offensive enough for parents to overtly object to it. This transgenerational audience-building strategy, combined with its combination of Indian and Western branding, enabled Channel V to claim a viewership of 12 million C/S households in 1997. Its successful run, however, was challenged at this time by the return of MTV.

MTV India began broadcasting in 1996, with a focus on defining and capturing an audience that would simultaneously be more "Indian" and young (Rawla & Hussain, 1997). It began to promote Indian pop music videos, as well as celebrity VJs of Indian and Indian/Western backgrounds. At the same time, for nearly one year after its return, MTV India avoided Hindi film music, in spite of its visibly "Indian" look in its promos. However, on August 1, 1997, MTV substantially increased its Indian branding, ostensibly in connection with India's Fiftieth Independence Day celebrations. The MTV logo appeared in the three colors of the Indian flag throughout the month, and Hindi film songs began to be featured in the programming in a substantial way. Soon, MTV India Director Sudanshu Sarronwala was claiming that "while only 30 percent of V's programming is Hindi, MTV has a breakup of 60 percent Hindi" (quoted in Rawla and Hussain, 1997). By 1999, MTV India had successfully established itself among young Indian audiences, particularly the 15–34 age group (Arathoon, 2000). In turn, Channel V announced that it would rethink its positioning, and make itself more youth-oriented (Hussain, 1999, March 3–9).

Although Channel V and MTV India have moved more directly toward a youth audience, the demands of the mass audience have continued to affect growth and competition in music television channels. The Zee network launched Music Asia in 1997, and quickly claimed as many as nine million potential viewing households ("Music Asia . . . ," 1997). Music Asia entered a void left by the frequent disappearances of another Indian music television channel ATN, which successfully promoted T-series cassettes but declared bankruptcy following the murder of T-series owner Gulshan Kumar. With the help of cross promotion from Zee, and its resolvedly Indian programming, Music Asia has laid claim to being the only Indian music television channel, and led to observations that Channel V and MTV India's Indianization strategies would soon have to be reexamined in response to the challenge from Music Asia (Rawla & Hussain, 1997). More recently, two more music television channels, B4U and ETC, have begun operations. The programming approaches of these channels remain focused on "family" and on being "Indian" ("Music is mantra . . . ," 2001; "Etc.," 2001).

The Music Industry

The rise of Indian music television, and the specific forms it has taken, are related not only to the global and national imperatives of liberalization, marketization, and audience building described thus far, but also to certain important developments in the Indian music industry that have been taking place since the 1980s. The close complicity between music television and the music industry is evident at the outset in the ownership patterns of music television at the global and national levels. In 1995, a substantial stake in Channel V was acquired by Sony, EMI, BMG, and Warner, which are four of the world's largest music corporations (Banks, 1996). In India, the music television channel ATN was owned and operated primarily for the promotion of the T-Series label until its murderous end, as mentioned earlier. Indian music television has also been spurred on by the vast potential of the Indian music market for global and domestic producers. In his study of the global music industry, Burnett (1996) points out that while the Indian music market may not have the same economic value as that in the United States and the West, its sheer size in terms of unit sales lends it some importance.

The Indian music industry, which has traditionally been largely dependent on the Indian film industry, began to acquire its own momentum thanks to the "cassette revolution" of the 1970s and economic liberalization in the 1980s, according to Manuel (1993). Despite a reported slowdown by the late 1990s after massive growth over the last two decades, it has certainly assumed an important role among media businesses in general (Mukherjee, 1997, May 23). At the same time, the industry, which was valued at $200 million in 1998, was expected to grow by at least a third of its value in the coming years ("Music Mania," 1998). Since the rise of satellite television, however, the Indian music business has been redefined by the enormous marketing potential of music television, even as it has also been at the center of a new emerging relationship between television and film.

From its beginnings as a colonialist enterprise in the early 1900s (Farrell, 1997), the Indian music industry's growth has largely followed that of the film industry, not in the least due to the fact that nearly every Indian film has been a musical. For its sheer popularity, Indian film music is described by Manuel (1993) as a "people's music" (p. 59). Film songs became important not only because of the roots of Indian cinema in musical stage forms, but also because prior to the "cassette revolution" of the 1970s, film was the main medium through which music was consumed. Although film music dominated music sales in the country, and still does, the record player and the record were not widely accessible outside the middle-classes. While radio was certainly more widespread in conveying film music to the masses, as Manuel (1993, p. 40) writes, it was also cautious in turning to film music (the popular *Vividh Bharathi* was established on All India Radio in 1957 only because radio audiences were tuning into Radio Ceylon for film music), and did not take away from film as the primary context for film songs.

Manuel (1993) demonstrates that the cassette revolution unleashed major changes in the Indian music industry, paralleled perhaps only by the impact of music television in recent years. The first wave of cassette technology came in during the 1970s when two-in-ones were brought back in large quantities by Indian workers in the Gulf countries, either for their own use or for sale on the black market. In addition, various Indian electronics manufacturers also began to produce cassette players, and GCI started issuing cassettes on a large scale. The cassette boom however took place in full force by the early 1980s, thanks to the government's easing of import restrictions on consumer electronic products. The government also began to encourage collaborations with foreign manufacturers, and numerous electronic brands such as Akai-Bush, Orson-Sony, and BPL-Sanyo began to emerge, in addition to collaborations in the area of magnetic tape production. By the mid-1980s, Manuel (1993, p. 63) reports, cassettes came to constitute 95 percent of the music market, as GCI's market share declined to about 15 percent in the face of the rise of at least 300 competitors—many of them local, "cottage-industry" operators.

Until this point, HMV had been a monopoly in the Indian music market. This was effectively ended by the rise of the somewhat shady label known as T-Series. T-Series began by issuing cover versions of Hindi film hits, reportedly at the request of the performers on occasion because HMV was unable to keep up with demand. In addition, it capitalized on the changing class composition of the music market by aggressively selling cassettes in places like *paan* (betel leaf) stalls and small grocery stores where working-class consumers could be reached. Although HMV still remained an important label, T-Series had occupied the film market by the late 1980s, accounting for 70 percent of all film music releases (Manuel, 1993).

In recent years, more companies have entered the music business. Music India Limited (MIL), a subsidiary of global music corporation Polygram, had entered the Indian market as early as 1969, and in spite of setbacks due to piracy in the 1980s, has since reestablished itself. MIL's strengths, unlike HMV and T-series, have been in international music, an area which saw numerous other labels emerge as well ranging from CBS in 1982 in collaboration with the Tata group to the label Magnasound which released, thanks to its tie-up with Warner, a long list of Western rock and pop albums beginning in 1989. More recently, Sony Music has also entered the Indian market, bringing in its international stars such as Aerosmith, and also promoting Indian pop.[9] In addition, various other companies have also emerged, some involving foreign tie-ups, such as Crescendo with BMG, as well as many more specializing in Indian film music, such as TIPS and Venus. Another successful entrant into the music business—although not necessarily via television—has been Music Today, a part of the Living Media Group which publishes the news magazine *India Today;* its repertoire includes Indian classical music, as well as themed albums that constitute what may be described as an Indian New Age sensibility.

In spite of the emergence of other genres in the music market, film music continues to remain important. Indian pop and international music were expected to grow from 5 percent and 6 percent respectively of the music market in 1995 to 15 percent and 21 percent in 2000, while the share of Indian film music was expected to decline from 76 percent to 51 percent according to an estimate from BMG-Crescendo (Agrawal, 1996). Film music remains an attractive proposition not only because of the fact that it would still constitute a substantial market, but also because of the high volume of sales involved. However, with the cost of film music rights ranging from Rs. 15–60 million ($300,000–$1.2 million), many music companies have ventured into film production; Polygram released the film *Khamoshi*, recovering one-third of its production costs on audio sales alone, and Gramco, HMV's film production wing, released *Sapne*, selling 15 million units in the audio market (Mukherjee, 1997, May 23).

Film Music in the Age of Music Television

Film producers increasingly demand for their investment in a movie the inclusion of a "mega song which . . . has a tenuous link with plot but a major effect at the box office" (Chopra, 1997, March 15). These mega songs or "item" songs, as they are sometimes called, are aimed at providing a spectacular experience to viewers with large numbers of dancers and outlandish and expensive sets. Producers claim to spend as much as 50 percent of their budget on these songs, and scripts for the films are often hastily assembled as an afterthought only after the songs have been conceived. To some extent, these trends are a continuation of changes in the Hindi film industry that began in the early 1980s because of a decline in audiences due to video piracy and an increasing reliance on underworld real estate financiers who raised the levels of investment—and the stakes for expected returns—substantially (Shah, 1997).

A more immediate reason, however, has been the growing role of the music industry in film as well as the dependence of both film and music producers on television for publicity. Music manufacturers reportedly pressure film producers to adopt the "six songs formula," including romantic, erotic, and "item" pieces, and with 60–65 percent of television programs in 79 channels reportedly being song-based, film producers are also anxious about getting through, given the increasingly competitive nature of advertising for films and music (Chopra, 1997, March 15). One fallout of this has been a substantial change in the nature of the film song itself, which draws heavily now from music videos and MTV-style aesthetics. This is not without its consequences for the more vulnerable members of the film industry; a recent trend in film songs has been the use of fashion models and foreign dancers—which usually means that the low-wage "extras" or "junior artists" who traditionally provided group support in film songs may have fewer opportunities.

Film songs have also begun to take on the music video format on television. While film songs constituted some of the most popular TV programs in the past (such as *Chitrahar*), these were often presented exactly as they were in the film, without embellishments by way of VJs, charts, or any other music television conventions. Since the countdown boom, however, film songs are seldom presented in their entirety on television, but reedited to work as videos or ads, which implies that while the soundtrack may belong to only one song, the visual may have scenes from different parts of the whole film. In addition, the rise of remix albums featuring film songs with added beats have also seen the rise of remix music videos, which combine film footage with new material.

Indian Pop and Music Videos

While film songs have thus begun to assume new forms in the new financial and technological climate, the music video has become essential to the nonfilm music industry as well. To some extent, this development underscores the close connections between the nascent Indian pop music industry and the growth of satellite television. Although Indian pop music has existed since at least since the 1970s in English and Hindi, it gained visibility and a market presence only in the 1990s. This is often attributed to the success of one music video, Alisha Chinai's *Made in India*, the first Indian pop album to register sales comparable to a film album, selling 2.2 million copies (not including pirated copies) when earlier nonfilm albums were considered to have been successful even if they sold 100,000 copies—underscoring at least one producer's perception that "Indian pop is here to stay" (quoted in Tellis & Frank, 1996).

While Indian pop has been useful for satellite channels in meeting their programming needs, it has also allowed music companies to take advantage of marketing through television. The emphasis, according to performers and music company executives, is on "packaging," with music videos constituting an important part of creating pop stars as a package. Pop performer Mehnaz attributes this to the fact that "Indian audiences love packaging," while "Lezz" Lewis of the pop duo Colonial Cousins is critical of too much emphasis on packaging by music companies (Tellis & Frank, 1996). Packaging is by no means restricted to publicity, but also implies what sort of musical genres are favored in Indian pop.

For instance, Indian English pop, which has had a small following since the 1970s, barely compares in terms of sales to Hindi Indian pop—or Western pop, for that matter. The rise in Hindi pop is also related to the new elite chic for all things Hindi, including films, which were earlier looked down upon by the upper classes. Musically, Hindi pop is also dominated by Bhangra-inspired styles, ranging from Daler Mehndi to the more juvenile themes of Baba Sahgal. With the possible exception of the

Colonial Cousins, whose music mixes Indian classical and film tunes with Western styles, most Indian pop music also follows the same formulae as Hindi film songs, such as hummable tunes and repeatable catchphrases.

Indian pop music videos also reflect the rather noncontroversial approach of the songs as well, avoiding, as in the case of Ken Ghosh, India's most prolific music video maker, the "angst ridden rebellion or even morbid sexuality so profuse in international videos" (Chopra, 1997, August 4, p. 81). Ken Ghosh, whose credits include Alisha's "Made in India" video, says he began in 1992 with Rs. 500 ($12) and is now worth Rs. 30 million ($800,000). His oeuvre has ranged from big-budget videos to many fly-by-night ones as well, but he is given credit for having helped to sell 80 million cassettes. His motto seems to be "It's easy to be arty. It's more difficult to make something that people like" (quoted in Chopra, 1997, August 4, p. 81).

Many music video producers tend to be advertising filmmakers by profession. Some music companies, like Polygram and T-Series, have their own music video production division, while others, for the most part, contract independent producers. On average, a music video costs as much as Rs. 1,000,000 ($25,000) to produce, while actual recording costs may be only a little over half that amount, according to Suresh Thomas, managing director of BMG Crescendo (quoted in Wagle, 1997). With the emphasis on releasing at least two videos from each album plus other publicity costs, each album entails an investment of about Rs. 2 million ($50,000), and needs to sell at least 200,000 units to break even. However, as is the case with the music industry in general, only 1 in 10 albums released actually becomes a hit, and often a hit is expected to recover the expected profits of the other albums as well.

It must be noted that there are far more music videos being produced than those that make it into widespread circulation on the countdowns. While the costs and profiles of these videos may not be on a high scale like those of some of the larger music companies, it is evident that numerous regional music companies are also involved in music video production even if these albums are not expected to sell as much as those by nationally established Indian pop stars.

* * *

It appears that the relative low profile of these videos allows more creative expression than the standard teenage love- and wedding-song format of many videos. For instance, one video on ATN features a futuristic scenario in which men and women's roles are interchanged, and shows an apron-clad husband meekly taking off his wife's shoes after work. Another video that appeared on Home TV in 1997 features outrageous stereotypes of South Indians. Music videos are certainly not absent from the regional music scene as well; for instance, Sun Music featured a music video called *Anandam* (joy) which shows teenagers with Ganesha masks cavorting on their motorbikes to an English/Carnatic pop version of *Vaatapi Gana Pathimpaje*, a traditional South Indian classical song.

In spite of the proliferation of music video production, there are also instances of performers who have had substantial commercial successes with little support from television, such as Altaf Raja. In addition, there are also various nonpop regional genres that have their own local fans without any publicity from television. The revolutionary folk songs of Gaddar, a former member of the Maoist Naxalite movement, are very successful in the state of Andhra Pradesh, especially among working-class people. His songs deal with class struggle and are critical of Indian and foreign capitalists.

However, the satellite television boom has changed the way music is marketed in India. While most music company executives are unanimous that music videos are the best form of publicity for their products—not in the least because they are displayed for free on television—there are also problems because of the proliferation of videos. There is a perception that "music videos have lost their effectivity due to the clutter on the channels" and are also replaced too frequently to be noticed, according to a Magnasound executive (quoted in Wagle, 1997, p. 33). Another concern is that with too much exposure on television, the impact of songs tends to wear out and consumers do not actually purchase the album—they are satisfied with just getting it for free on television. All the same, music companies clearly need the publicity of television, especially in the pop market, and there has been no shortage of high-budget music videos as well in recent years.

Music television has also changed the way consumers purchase music. In spite of the persistence of piracy, it appears that consumers find it more convenient to purchase albums rather than simply record selected tracks from one another (or from stores). As one journalist points out, it has become common for people to purchase a whole album on the strength of one or two songs, and oftentimes without even listening to selections in the music store (Moses, 1995). Music retailers also say that there has been a change in the way people make purchases. In the past, there was a need for salespeople to talk to customers at great length about the music and play selections, but since the advent of music television customers walk in with a clear idea of what they want to purchase.

Music Television Audiences in Context

Changes in consumption practices are however only a small portion of the impact of music television in India. While I consider the implications of this impact in the rest of this book, it is worth noting the place of music television and its audiences in the broader political economy. The music television audience in India is not a homogenous and coherent entity. It may be located at the intersection of a broad negotiation by media businesses between the demands of mass and niche audiences defined in terms of class, language, and age. Access to satellite television is circumscribed, at the outset, not only by the costs of television ownership and cable subscription (which was around Rs. 150 or $3.50 per month at the time of this study), but also by the technical capabilities of the television set (not all sets are color, or capable of receiving many channels). In addition, cable operators in low-income neighborhoods may or may not provide channels like MTV.

Although television viewing may not necessarily be an elite phenomenon, it is worth asking who the Indian audience actually is. Even if the "great Indian middle class" that has spurred on satellite television and liberalization[10] is only 100 million strong (as opposed to the mythical figure of 250 million), the question does remain as to who the rest of the 900 million people are. Television has indeed become affordable to a greater number of people than in the past thanks to hire-purchase schemes. It is not unusual for many low-income families—especially in urban areas—to own a television set. However, the commercialization of television has had an especially harsh impact on these families as noted by Sevanti Ninan (1995). The patronizing assumption often heard in debates about globalization that the poor would be motivated to work harder by commercial television is belied by the fact that all that poor viewers seem to do in response to television is cut back on their regular food so their children can have that one expensive chocolate advertised on television (Ninan, 1995).

India's 55 million TV households[11] are segmented in terms of location and class. At the time of this study, only 15 million TV households had access to cable and satellite (C/S) channels, and as mentioned earlier, many C/S households may not even have technological access to the full assortment of these channels.[12] The urban-rural divide is especially pronounced in the case of satellite television. While as much as 20 percent of the rural population reportedly has been "penetrated" by television (Doordarshan), only 2–3 percent of the rural population has C/S connections; which in terms of TV households would translate to 22 million rural television households and only about 2 million rural C/S households ("A Peek into Rural Viewership," 1997). In addition, the spread of TV in rural areas has been highest in certain affluent states, including Andhra Pradesh, and is also restricted to rural elites such as landowners. Finally, C/S reception in rural areas has also been restricted mainly to South India, with the Telugu channel ETV and the Tamil channel Sun being the leaders. Thus, the satellite TV boom of Star, MTV, and even Zee TV does not have much rural resonance; cable operators in rural areas often provide no more than one or two channels to subscribers.

At the same time, the TV boom has resulted in substantial changes in the viewing habits and daily lives of viewers. The National Readership Survey (NRS), perhaps the most exhaustive study of urban Indian media markets, reports major increases in TV viewing in its reports of both 1995 and 1997 ("Couch Potatoes on the Rise," 1998). The percentage of those who rarely watch TV fell from 23 percent in 1990 (before the satellite boom) to about 7 percent in 1995, and those of heavy viewers (over 3 hours a day) rose from less than 3 percent to close to 10 percent. Interestingly, Sunday viewing also dropped by 1995, indicating not only that people were not bound to the Doordarshan Sunday movie as they were in the past, but also that they were "going out" for recreation.

Television viewing has thus certainly become a greater part of daily life for many people since satellite television was introduced—an average viewer in 1997 spent 13 hours per week on TV, an increase of two hours per week since 1995. On this note, while "audiencehood" may be seen as an increasingly pervasive condition of Indian life, the question about its role in the larger economy still remains. Interestingly, NRS-V, which reported an increase in all income groups in the city in 1995, also shows that the largest growth among all income groups took place in Group "E," consisting of families with incomes of less than Rs. 750 ($18) per month. Also, only 13 percent of Group "E" families live in the larger cities, and as much as 50 percent of them live in small towns (population less than 100,000) pointing toward an urban-rural disparity.

Television is situated in an economy which under liberalization results in a sharp polarization in the social distribution of privileges and costs in societies. As Kurien (1994) writes, an economy is a "social institution" and hence not something natural or inevitable. In concrete terms, what liberalization entails is a relinquishing to the market of social responsibility for the majority of the Indian population, which includes agricultural laborers, small farmers, and informal and household workers and their families. These are the people for whom the market is not a happy purveyor of music videos and Levi's jeans, but is instead a "tool of oppression" which has intruded and destroyed their traditional sources of livelihood through the larger marketization and monetization of the economy.

The television audience in India, especially in its more globalized forms since the advent of satellite television, must therefore be seen as the historically situated outcome of specific social and political choices and investments that have shaped the broader economy at the national and global levels. It is important, therefore, to conceive of television as being situated in the same economy, or set of social and material relations, that simultaneously make its lifestyle celebration possible even as livelihood becomes impossible for another constituency. However, one irony in this process is that the privatization and marketization of television have been sanctioned as a process of enfranchising the public. In an important legal ruling in a case between Doordarshan and private broadcasters over broadcasting rights to the Hero Cup cricket tournament in 1995, the Supreme Court actually turned the normally understood notions of "public" and "private" (referring to state and market, as in the West) on their head by declaring that broadcasting should be accessible to the public, *and therefore*, to private broadcasters (Agrawal & Mukhopadhyay, 1997). Private broadcasters and Doordarshan in its new commercial zeal are, in spite of their celebrations of the "public" in all manners (as I will show in Chapter 3), bound in their functioning to cater not to the public in any broad sense, but only to those who are considered to be of value to them in economic terms. This, in the first instance, determines all that music television audiences have become.

CHAPTER 2

MUSIC TELEVISION AND ITS AUDIENCES

We watch all the songs, wherever we find them, we watch them.
—A participant

You're in it!
—Channel V promo

In this chapter, I turn to some of the semiotic issues and consequences in the reception of music television in India. It is worth emphasizing that these consequences pertain not only to the broader location of the audience in the social relations between the consumer sector and everyone else as discussed in the previous chapter, but also to the subjects of this study, those who have indeed become audiences. In this chapter, I examine what music television and being a music television audience mean for the participants in this study. It would be fair to say at the outset that neither of these terms have relevance in themselves for these participants. In other words, participants do not necessarily think of music television as "music television," or of themselves as "viewers" of music television in the manner that one may expect the mythical global teenage MTV viewer to. Their engagement with the programs, songs, and conventions of all that constitutes music television in India is prioritized around certain elements and themes, and self-consciously being an "MTV Fan," for instance, is not one of them. These elements include, most importantly, the film songs and music videos, as well as an emerging sense of recognition of the new conventions and forms of mediation that go along with them.

Implicit in this argument is the patterns of continuities and differences between the practices of watching music television in the present global context, and those of watching film songs on television in the presatellite television era. I argue in this chapter that although participants do not explicitly stake a new identity for themselves as music television viewers, they are indeed negotiating not only the familiar pleasures of watching film songs, but the many new curiosities and conventions of present-day music television. For the most part, this negotiation seems to be a process of normalization, of new ways of watching film songs, music videos, and of course, music television in general. In this chapter, I discuss some of the main dimensions along which watching music television is normalized: the seeking by participants of something more than music in these programs (often referred to as "attitude"), the demands placed by them on VJs for a certain kind of authenticity (demands that are interestingly not made of musicians here), and finally, their tentative explorations of the meanings of visual practices in relation to music television and an emerging sense of generational identity. The result of these processes, as I explore in later chapters, is that there is at the outset a broad epistemic position that has come into social existence in relation to the discursive demands of music television; and audiences, albeit in different ways, have come to occupy this.

Watching Music Television

Despite the tradition of watching film songs on television in India, the reception of contemporary music television as seen in this study is marked by emerging practices pertaining to attention, interest, recall, knowledge, taste, and investment that are inflected on the basis of class and age. The distribution of viewing preferences among participants is quite similar to local and national television rating figures, with Indian language film countdowns clearly ahead of Western or Indian pop music countdowns, highlighting issues of not only interest but also access. At the outset, the 42 participants in this study had different degrees of access to television. For instance, five of them indicated that they had only television but not a cable/satellite connection. Even among those who had cable/satellite, there were variations in the number of channels their sets were capable of receiving. Only one participant indicated that her set was capable of receiving more than 20 channels. As mentioned in the earlier chapter, these technical constraints of television access are indicative of the larger population as well. However, the lack of unrestrained access to the full range of available satellite channels does not preclude familiarity with them. Although some participants did not recall countdown shows outside those on Doordarshan, many of them who did not have cable/satellite access at home were certainly aware of the shows on popular cable/satellite channels such as Zee TV.

The most frequent responses to the first, open-ended question of the interviews, "What countdown shows can you name?" were Doordarshan's *Superhit Muqabla* (9), Gemini's *Santoor Top Ten* (9) and Zee TV's *Philips Top Ten* (7). It is worth emphasizing that these are all film music-based countdown shows. In comparison, there were no more than two responses for any of the pop music-based shows, such as Channel V's *Indian Top Ten* and Sony's *Take Five*. The international countdowns, such as *Asian Top Twenty* and *Billboard* U.S. charts were mentioned by no more than two participants. In addition, there were a number of other shows that were mentioned—but not by a large number of participants. These include *Public Demand*, *Ek Se Badkar Ek*, *Ikke pe Ikka*, *Top of the Tops*, *Superhit Hungama*, and *Priyaragalu*. Once again, the distribution of familiarity with countdown shows among the participants in this study does not contradict broader ratings as well. *Superhit Muqabla* and *Philips Top Ten* have some of the highest nationwide ratings for TV in general and cable/satellite TV in particular respectively. While *Santoor Top Ten* does not figure in the national ratings since it is a regional language show, it is highly rated at the local and state levels.

Participants' familiarity with and liking for programs and specific songs follows some patterns in terms of demographic distribution, despite the spread of most film music across class and age. The main difference is the fact that music countdowns and the various conventions of music television are largely the forte of middle-class participants and particularly middle-class participants under 30. However, a great deal of the music is watched by older middle-class participants and working-class participants as well. Even among middle-class participants, genre recognition and program recall are not uniform. "Countdown" was sometimes taken by participants to mean any program with music, and shows such as *Antakshari* were mentioned. But on prompting and clarification ("a countdown is a show in which songs are ranked"), many younger middle-class participants were on target in their recollection. Also, many participants indicated that they seldom watch countdown shows in their entirety, looking instead for either songs they like or the top songs on the chart. One person did point out that this was a new development, and in the early days of satellite television (the early 1990s) it was more common for people to watch shows in their entirety.

At this point, it would be useful to address the centrality of the musical content of music television programs in terms of the tastes of the participants in this study. The specific programs watched by participants clearly indicate the relative marginality of Western pop music videos and programs in general, and the strong appeal of Indian film music across class and generational lines. To illustrate, only 9 instances (performers and songs) of Western pop songs are mentioned (and mostly by members of two groups), in comparison with 17 instances (films and songs) for Hindi films and 12 instances for Telugu films. While film songs are referenced across generational and class lines among participants, there are some indications of how references to other kinds of music, including Indian pop, remixes, and nonpop international/fusion are segmented along class and generational lines.[1] It is mainly the upper levels of the middle-class participants who indicate a keen interest in and knowledge of international performers such as the Spice Girls, Boyzone, and Guns and Roses. Although some Western performers like Michael Jackson are mentioned by middle-class participants, their interests are mainly in current Hindi and Telugu films songs and in Indian pop music. Fusion and world music performers such as Khaled (from Algeria) and Nusrat Fateh Ali Khan (from Pakistan) are mentioned exclusively by older middle-class participants with high educational capital (postdoctoral researchers). Other graduate-level middle-class students indicate an interest in both Western classical music and South Indian classical music. Some participants also indicate that there are some forms of music that they do not like at all, such as "Techno" (a term used by a participant who is otherwise a fan of Western pop) and "Rap" (used in this case by a middle-class graduate student as a criticism of obscenity in Indian film music).

Among the working-class participants, the children mention Hindi and Telugu films, while the parents like Telugu films such as *Ose Ramulamma* and *Singanna*, both of which deal sympathetically with the Naxalite movement of Andhra Pradesh. In addition, while participants also offer generic descriptions about the kind of music they like, there are also differences in genre competences. For instance, some categories that are mentioned have more to do with ways of expressing personal taste rather than genres as such (with the exception of "dance music," which is also a successful compilation-driven genre in the Indian music market). These include "old songs," "soft songs," "songs you can dance with," and "songs with inspiring lyrics." Older middle-class viewers, however, only mention old Telugu film songs such as "Jagame Maya" from *Devadas* and "Vivaha Bhojanambu" from *Maya Bazaar* as their favorites, although they are also familiar with current film songs.

While these categories are useful as indicators of participants' tastes and abilities to express their relationship to music and television, the full import of the reception of music television is better appreciated by turning to the broader theoretical question of the relationship between music and music television. First of all, it is worth noting that "music" is in some ways a historically arbitrary construction that carries its own sense of borders and rules, which are evident in the ways in which participants describe different kinds of music. As Simon Frith (1996) puts it, "Music becomes music by being heard as such by the listener" (p. 100). Frith's point is not so much that music lacks innate or inherent qualities in terms of the organization of sounds, but the fact that these organized sounds are recognized as music in the contexts of modern life, and the social basis for such recognitions to be made is also a political one.[2] In this sense, the history of music technology, including the articulation in India of the "film song" and the "music video," may be seen in terms of how power is organized and reorganized in society. Thus, Jody Berland (1993) compares the invention of music video in the early 1980s to that of recording technology earlier in the century. What recording technologies do, at the very least, is enable the separation of music from the performer's body, and thus from the place in which music is produced. Berland locates the separation of music from place in the broader "history of production, not of things, but of space" (p. 27) and describes the role of the music video, as "present(ing) itself as representing . . . what it is also displacing: the social context of the music itself" (p. 27).

Although, as mentioned earlier, neither film songs nor the more recent Indian pop music have the same sort of ties to "place" to begin with, and are both essentially studio creations, what is relevant here is the ways in which the conventions of music television since 1991 have changed the experience of music as both an aural and a visual form, and what music may have done to change the experience of television, as well. Berland argues that music video represents nothing less than "cultural cannibalization" (p. 37) in the consumption of music by image. While this criticism is certainly relevant, it needs further development, given the empirical and theoretical challenges presented by the complexities of music television. Such an argument is found in Andrew Goodwin's (1992) discussion of MTV. While neither Goodwin nor Berland are celebratory of music television in general, Goodwin's discussion of music television emphasizes the fact that music television needs to be understood on its own terms, and not so much as a mere visual appendage to something with an *a priori* existence as "music." Thus, for Goodwin, "music video is relatively autonomous from the music" (p. 85), and music television is better understood as television being "musiced" rather than the other way around. The film songs and music videos that participants mention in this study may therefore be seen as relatively autonomous from the music itself, and such a move would be useful in posing the main question in this context not so much in terms of viewers' reactions to visualization as a form of mediating music, but in terms of music television in general as a sphere of broader social mediations.

Goodwin's position is generally supported in this study by the absence of any comparisons between music and music videos in terms of the representation of the former in the latter. Although some participants express limitations to the concept of "watching music"—for instance, that certain musical genres are not appropriate for being visualized—it is significant that music television in general is not perceived as secondary to a more authentic, aural, "music." It would therefore be fair to say that despite the somewhat understated sense of self-consciousness as a music television audience among participants, it is evident that they are indeed, in the manner of their engagements with the conventions and practices of music television, situated in a social and discursive condition that is a form of music television audiencehood. It is this condition from which, as I show in the later chapters, a deeper sense of self (and self-consciousness) is emerging in India. In other words, watching music television, and particularly understanding the meaning of music television, suggests a process of normalization of various practices and conventions that are arguably specific to television under the immediate historic context of liberalization and globalization. The term "normalization" is not used to imply here that participants do not question, challenge, or criticize music television in the interviews. What is more important is the fact that certain features associated with music television in contemporary India that clearly did not exist prior to the satellite television boom are not mentioned as being problematic or unusual in any significant way by participants. This is not to say that participants have not noticed the new forms and conventions of music television. It may well be the case that music television is submerged in the sense of inevitability of its new forms. As one participant, a middle-class college student, says: "It's television, and it has to go on."

This statement provides a useful sense of the overall tone in which the question of normalization may be approached. On the one hand, this participant does find something problematic about music television, and that his parents have reason to find something problematic; but he also assumes a pragmatic position by saying that there is not much that he thinks that can be done to stop the march of television—a position that may be usefully contrasted with the opinion expressed by some other participants who see the growth of television as broadening career opportunities for them in arts and marketing. In general, however, the perceptions of music television indicate little sense of a total opposition to it, although there are occasional criticisms of the music, and the broader creative concepts within which the music is framed in the video. At the beginning of each interview, participants were asked to compare the new countdowns with *Chitrahar* (which presented film songs with little emphasis on fillers or graphics). The following statement by a postgraduate reseacher and computer entrepreneur suggests an important form of articulation in the reception of music television in India; that of the "technically" desirable "new programs" and the implicit authenticity and aesthetic value of Indian film songs:

> Technically, these new programs are much better than *Chitrahar*. But these also have an imitative style. The songs were very good in *Chitrahar*. Melodies. (Praveen)

This participant indicates that the "technical" aspects of the new programs are indeed discernible, and much better than those in *Chitrahar*. At the same time, he is also critical of the lack of originality among the new programs, and mentions that *Chitrahar* was unique and characterized by a better range of songs. This notion of *Chitrahar* as representing something more genuine or pleasurable in terms of its music selection, as well as its no-frills character, are mentioned quite positively by another participant, a recent college graduate. He is in fact quite unimpressed by the fact that *Chitrahar* had recently undergone a substantial revision in its presentation to make it more appropriate to the contemporary televisual context. Another participant says:

> Actually, in the attempt to catch up with the other countdown, they're spoiling the show. The thing is that previously, they would show us songs and less of talking things. Now it is basically that Javed Jaffrey keeps on talking. . . . They're all rubbish sometimes, the in between talk that is produced, it has no sense. He tries to like just create some people to laugh but he's not able to do that. *Chitrahar* is not able to get the background like *BPL Oye* or any other countdown. (Arun)

This participant is not necessarily a critic of countdowns, but sees *Chitrahar*'s attempts to change its format as imitative, and unsuccessfully so at that. He seems to think that there is room on television for songs to be enjoyed without all the embellishments of countdowns, and echoes a criticism raised by many other participants about the lack of adequate airtime and attention for the song itself on countdowns. Thus, while there is a perception that songs are important, and that countdowns may not do justice to viewers' interest in seeing more of songs and less of fillers, this does not imply that this participant is opposed to the concept of what he calls the "background." As he goes on to explain:

> If you want something different, not just the songs [then countdowns are good]. Like Masala Mix in *BPL Oye*, something like that, attitude it creates. *Chitrahar* is just a countdown. Okay. Ordinary countdown. We don't get it on MTV, we watch it on Doordarshan. (Arun)

According to him, the countdown can be very entertaining for viewers who are interested in something more than the songs. Although, for instance, the VJ Javed Jaffrey is criticized here because he "keeps on talking" at the expense of the songs on *Chitrahar*, he is regarded well by the majority of participants. Countdowns, MTV's countdowns in particular, are seen as being attractive because of their "background" and "attitude,"[3] and for being "something different." These terms show audience familiarity with some of the new conventions of music television—and desire for these conventions as well.

To illustrate, using the example mentioned above, "Masala Mix" is a nonchart section of Channel V's *BPL Oye* in which a creative hodgepodge of imagery and music is presented in the form of a contest. For instance, around the time that the interview took place, the Masala Mix featured a George Michael video reedited to match the soundtrack of a Hindi film song with remarkable timing so as to simulate almost perfect lip-synching. While the production of "attitude" is by no means confined to the pleasures of watching George Michael appear to sing an Indian film song in place of his own lyrics, other examples of a similar form of ingenuity in adapting Western music videos abound as well. To some extent, the notion of attitude is thus related to the creative ways in which music television can express the Indian-Western hybridity that media planners think is very chic among young Indians (Hussain, 1999, February 10–16).

This participant's comments indicate that viewers of music television expect to be entertained not only by the songs, but also by the unexpected, playful, or mildly subversive. The fact that songs are considered important as well, however, indicates that there may be various standards of judgments being used by viewers in deciding when the filler becomes distracting or intolerable. In other words, the various creative touches that viewers get in addition to the song (sometimes within the context of the song itself, as seen in the examples above), may sometimes be deemed entertaining, but also run the risk of being criticized for taking time away from the music.

Despite the presence of such negotiations of relevance between music and fillers, what is important is the fact that there may be an emerging sense of normalization that has emerged around the new practices that surround the presentation of songs on television. Although audiences in the past may have been quite satisfied with *Chitrahar*'s presentation of songs without much introduction or fanfare, in the new context, even the thought of the absence of such conventions seems to be confounding. As Arun says: "We can't go directly into the song. It looks very odd."

While this participant, a high school student, is critical elsewhere in the interview of the way some VJs act, his comment illustrates his acceptance of one of the premises on which music television is structured at the very level of intelligibility. When he says that one cannot do without introductions and other fillers between songs, he is indicating what is "normal" to him in music television. Other participants also indicate their tacit support for such a position, but in different ways, and mostly in relation to the role of VJs. Some say that the information given by VJs is important, while others say that they watch certain programs mainly because they like the VJs. In general, these perceptions are related to how VJs fit into the broader theme of the program, or what one participant calls the "anchoring concepts."

VJs and Acting Naturally

One important aspect of the normalization of music television conventions is the way in which participants negotiate their likes and dislikes for the VJ. The figure of the VJ seems to be central to how younger middle-class participants watch music television, and there was no dearth of interest and investment in talking about one's favorite VJ during the interviews. In fact, it seemed as if the VJ was a more popular kind of celebrity for them than any pop singer or musician. Older middle-class participants, however, knew the names of the hosts and presenters among the more popular programs on channels like Doordarshan and Zee, but did not necessarily identify with the MTV or Channel V VJ in the manner that younger participants did. Working-class participants, in general, did not have much knowledge or interest in the VJ.

For young participants, the relevance of the VJ seems to be deeply in-

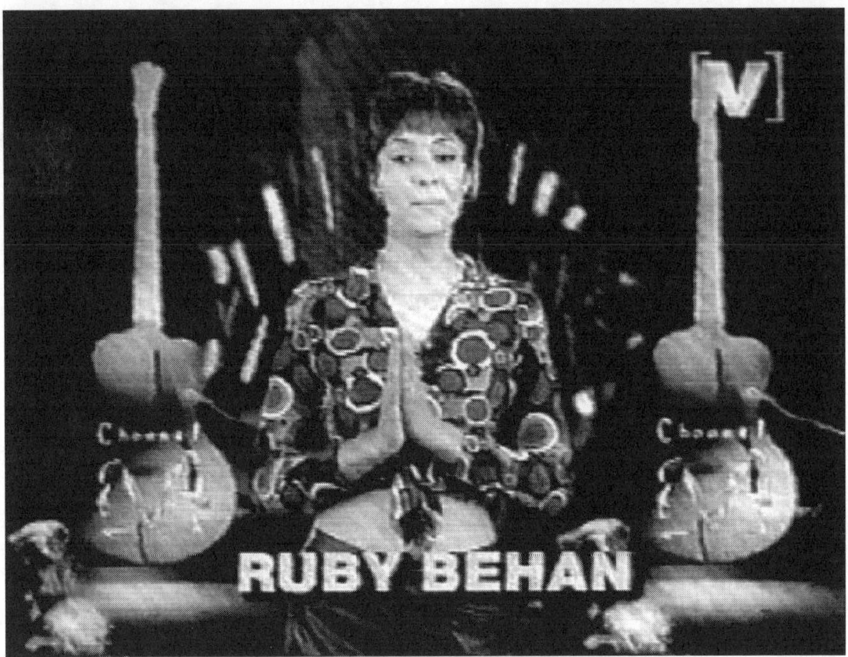

FIGURE 3 VJ Ruby in a self-consciously "ethnic" moment on the Indian Top Ten.

grained, and it is not only the presence of the VJ in music television which has been normalized, but the assumption that one would have to have a favorite VJ as well. One participant, for instance, responded with remarkable readiness when asked if there was any VJ he particularly liked (Arun): "My VJ is Rahul. He's a cool guy."

The ready response of this participant with regard to favorite VJs may be contrasted with the fact that questions about "favorite" singers seldom drew such a quick response. Although it does not imply that participants do not know the names of singers or bands, it is significant that talking about popular music during the interviews revolved more around the names of specific songs, or the films in which these songs appeared, than around the names of singers. This may be an indication of the relative lack of emphasis on musical authorship in Indian popular music. As mentioned earlier, the prevalence of playback singing in Indian film music has meant that despite their popularity, playback singers and film music composers are seldom celebrated as "stars" in the same manner as Western pop singers are, although this trend has begun to change somewhat with their appearance in music videos and massive televised concerts.

In contrast, VJs, especially those on Channel V and MTV, appear to carry certain burdens of celebrity and authenticity among viewers in a way that musicians do not. For example, no participants talked about musicians' responsibility towards being "authentic" or representative to their idiom or to fans' expectations—although these are important issues in pop music in general (Frith, 1996) and often get especially politicized in certain genres like World Music (Taylor, 1997). In other words, apparently no participant expects Alisha Chinai, the Colonial Cousins, or A. R. Rahman to define and remain true to their musical roots, while many participants express their views of how VJs should and should not be.

This may be a sign of a disjuncture between the cultures of music and music television in India. While film music has been immensely popular, it has arguably not been at the center of a musical culture in the same way as rock music in the West has. The more recent Indian pop music culture, too, has few mandates to fulfill in terms of its origins, and is by and large a studio-driven phenomenon as well. It appears then that the role of situating music in a youth-friendly pop culture falls mainly to music television, and particularly the international music television channels. Thus, it is clear that participants are not evaluating VJs as any old sort of "TV announcers," but as celebrities who are an integral part of the new television-driven Indian pop culture.

Some programs are favored by participants mainly because of their interest in the VJs. Although one participant says that a VJ is not strictly necessary for a countdown on principle, the obvious admiration with which many VJs who have their own programs are mentioned by a number of participants indicates that VJs have their own zone of relative autonomy in the successful reception of music television programs. For instance, Channel V's Trey, who is mentioned by a number of participants as their favorite VJ, is known for certain antics with which participants keep up, such as the escapades he has with his puppet sidekick "Muriel." Channel V and MTV VJs are in a sense cultivated as celebrities by the channels through extensive promos and hype—and often get adoring letters and phone calls on their request shows from people who appear to be young teenagers from across Asia. However, there is a somewhat different set of hosts and VJs in music television programs that are not necessarily promoted as celebrities but are very popular as well. Older participants in particular mention music program hosts like Javed Jaffrey, Roshan Abbas, and Sajid Khan, as performers they like to watch. These examples may indicate that participants, especially older ones, are able to relate to the role of the music television presenter in ways different from the VJ-centered one of Channel V and MTV as well. Outside of the somewhat hysterical publicity which often surrounds popular personalities from Channel V and MTV (MTV's Cyrus was a favorite of the media around the time of this study), there are some clear ideas that audiences may have about what makes a VJ authentic, or simply "natural."

These ideas are apparent in the severe criticisms that some participants, especially those who are not necessarily regular viewers of Channel V and MTV, express. The following comments, for instance, come from two participants who are postgraduate dance students and mainly viewers of regional language channels:

> Actually the trend should change. Regarding the anchoring and all. Because each and every channel people are always imitating each other. They're not trying to change, their own way, they're always trying to imitate the other channel. So I feel they should be changing the way they are presenting. People are getting bored, always, the way they speak and their body language, their mannerisms and all. (Kamala)

> For example, the Zee TV people are trying to imitate V Channel people. The Telugu anchors are trying to imitate Hindi anchors and all. It is artificial. (Lakshmi)

These participants may or may not have a problem with VJs on the international channels, but find the ways in which many VJs on the other channels behave somewhat crude and imitative. This perhaps reveals some inflections and limits to the normalization of music television at various geocultural levels. What may seem fairly cool on MTV, for instance, could be seen as being cheaply offensive on another channel. It does not even seem to be the case that viewers would have to have access to MTV in the first place to be able to then criticize the other channels for their lack of originality, as is the case with the above participants.

The main problem with VJs on other channels, as they point out, is that they are part of a derivative hierarchy, in which regional channels imitate the national channels, which in turn imitate the international ones. The result of this lack of originality is apparent in the way they speak, their mannerisms, and their overall lack of restraint, which comes across as being "artificial." One term that is used frequently by participants to criticize VJs, is that they "overact,"[4]—which suggests that the problem with VJs is not seen as one of authenticity alone, but also one of good taste and decorum, which are generally noticeably lacking.

At the same time, some participants—especially those who are also familiar with the international channels—have a sense of what they expect from a good VJ. As the following comment suggests, there is certainly an expectation that VJs are not mere presenters who introduce songs, but are instead performers who:

> should be able to express [something] different from life. Something that is unnatural, something like that, different from our formal life. So he must be able to express those things easily. (Samir)

Thus, VJs are expected, by at least some participants, to express the "unnatural" in the sense of the unexpected, but at the same time this is perceived as being successful only if the performance does justice to the creative concepts or the script:

> They should be like a realist in [presenting] . . . though it is a preplanned joke, it should be presented as if it is spontaneous. And that looks good. (Arun)

VJs are hence expected to be different, but also realistic. In other words, the creative departures from routine presentations and ideas are welcomed by viewers, but these are considered entertaining only if the presentation comes across as "spontaneous." On that note, Pratibha, another participant, who is also a regular viewer of Channel V and MTV, offers the following prescription: "Just be yourself. Don't try too hard."

The notion of a VJ being "natural" or being oneself, as opposed to "overacting," may be seen as another instance of the normalization of music television practices in the Indian context. While viewers may not necessarily think that a VJ is anything but a performer working off a script, they express the expectation that a VJ would have to appear natural or spontaneous in doing that. However, the assumption that VJs' naturalness is only an effect of their acting talents cannot be easily overstated, given the fact that being natural is a persistent theme in many of the above comments. In other words, there are clearly some things about what VJs say, do, or wear, that allows viewers to assume that they are being natural or being "themselves."

How VJs can be themselves is a tricky issue, especially given the challenge of multiple languages and affectations in an environment of fashionable and self-conscious hybridity. In what has become a pervasive trend, both Channel V and MTV India feature a number of foreign-born or biracial Indian VJs—ostensibly to come across as "Indian" in some ways and "international" in others. A number of VJs are used to signify being "Indian" through their names, heritage, and perhaps the color of their skin in a manner that Melissa Butcher (1999) describes as "contortions of idealised nationhood" (p. 177). When these VJs speak, however, they come across as distinctly North American or British. On a similar note, it is also interesting that in spite of all the Indianization claims of the international channels, many announcements and promo voice-overs are delivered by non-Indian English speakers—constructing a thrill for viewers perhaps of having Indian names exoticized by a foreign accent (this claim may be further supported by the discussion in Chapter 4).

In spite of the pervasiveness of this phenomenon, it is interesting that this point was not mentioned by participants during their discussion of VJs, except when prompted. The following comments illustrate two broad and somewhat opposing positions. During the first interview, two participants, both high school students fairly familiar with a wide range of channels, expressed their criticism about "fake" accents—but only when I raised the issue:

> See, it's like most of the VJs are Indian. You know, Rahul Khanna or Tarun. Most of them are Indian, they fake the accent. (Mamatha)

> Many of them put on an accent. They don't have it originally. So the thing looks quite artificial. (Nisha)

Some VJs may not necessarily be putting on a "fake" accent, since they may have been raised in the West. What is important, however, is the fact that the presence of Indian-looking foreign-sounding VJs is in general not problematized by participants, and it is perhaps only calling attention to it that seems to provoke criticism. In other words, the issue here is how such a particular representation of being Indian and international at the same time is in a sense normalized in reception. For instance, one group of participants, who were perhaps the most Channel V- and MTV-savvy ones, shouted along word for word when a Channel V promo (an excerpt from which is quoted at the beginning of this chapter) was being shown in the interview—with the American accent intact.

For another participant, however, the intrusion of my question about the normalcy of these accents on television provided an opportunity for a suitably well-imagined response:

> As far as catering [to] the public is concerned, I think they have to do that. If they are going to talk in English accent [or] Indian accent, I don't think Thailand people or Philippines people are going to follow it . . . because it's basically Asian channel, not Indian channel. People mind that. (Vijay)

For this participant, a postgraduate researcher, the foreign accents of certain channels seem to be justified by the fact that these channels are catering to an Asian audience, as opposed to an exclusively Indian one. The imagined presence of viewers in other nations allows him to make this claim while simultaneously this claim may enable such an imaginative constitution to take place. Even as the normalization of accents in this case feeds into an emerging sensibility about location and identification as a global audience that I examine further in Chapter 4, another broad area of normalization is worth examining here, that of the fundamentally visual nature of music television. In addition to the demographic variations in tastes in music and investment in the persona of the VJ discussed so far, the visualization of music television seems to be especially rooted in generational issues, and may be the key aspect of music television around which a self-conscious youth culture may be being negotiated.

Youthful Looks

The negotiated acceptance of some of the conventions of music television described above by viewers may be further understood as a form of normalization in relation to the spread of a wider sensibility about being able to watch music as well as listen to it. In other words, the normalization of some of these conventions may be embedded in a process that may be characterized as a normalization of looking. Given the history of film as an important context for music in India, this process does not necessarily mean that there has been a sudden sensory shift in the experience of music because of music television.

Instead, the visualization of music and the intersections of film songs with television culture may be seen as part of the larger emergence of visual discourse through the proliferation of technology. The proliferation of television channels essentially means more things for audiences to look at, and also implies the rise of certain ideological claims that a culture of looking carries. For instance, many new programs connote a process of seeking the truth through looking, and the fragmented imagery of music television fillers and promos often consists of cameras, televisions, and computer monitors. In one sense, all these images may serve to reinforce the dominance of sight as a privileged way of knowledge under modernity to the extent that, as Chris Jenks (1995) says, "only that which can be 'seen' can be believed" (p. 6). In concrete terms, what this means may also be appreciated in the fact that television cameras—not in the least by virtue of the proliferation of television in general—have entered places and events in recent years that seldom, if ever, found representation in visual media in general and television in particular prior to the satellite television boom.

The vast increase in real and imaginary spaces that are brought into visualized representation on television presupposes an absence of contestation for such a sweeping scope for the camera in India. The scope of the television camera ranges from its newfound ability to focus on politicians who willingly participate in popular "mock trial" programs to the increasing presence of local and everyday people and events, especially on local cable channels. In between these examples is, of course, the vast amount of programming that uses everyday public spaces likes shopping centers and city streets either as active settings (such as public interviews) or as backgrounds.

A scopic increase of such magnitude surely must come up with some limitations, at the very least in terms of what is considered acceptable to be "seen" on television. One such limitation that is apparent among participants in this study is that of generational identity. At the outset, the descriptions of intergenerational negotiations of television viewing in their homes made by some participants point to questions about what is considered acceptable to look at. For instance, one participant recounts that her mother finds a particular MTV promo offensive because it shows a man expectorating *paan*-juice on to the camera lens, and by extension, the viewer's face.

More frequently, though, notions of control over what may or may not be seen revolve around issues of nudity, intimacy, and vulgarity. Although some participants say they sometimes feel uncomfortable when obscene images appear on television and their parents are in the room, few participants say that their parents had problems with their watching music television programs. The only contention they had with their parents with regard to television, they say, related for the most part to the choice of what channels to watch, because parents either wanted to watch BBC or the regional language channels. In general, there seems to be no indication from young participants that parents actively regulated or intervened in participants' viewing of music television—although one participant mentioned that while her parents did not mind MTV, her grandparents, who lived with them, found it objectionable. In the only interview in which parents and children participated together, the working-class mothers present said that they did not have issues with obscenity on television, but were more concerned that their children would not do their homework if they watched too much television.

Among the younger middle-class participants, in one of the few instances in the interviews in which parental objections to watching music television were mentioned, these objections were qualified in the following manner:

> Like, I can watch with my father, but I can't watch with my mother. And my friends also. They can watch with one parent but they can't watch with the other because . . . like your mothers don't accept all this. Fathers are a bit okay, they'll say, okay, fine, this is how it is, come on. (Arun)

In addition to the gender difference that this participant (a young man newly out of college) articulates, there is also a perception that the rules about what may or may not be seen are rooted in a national sensibility:

> It differs from family to family I think. Some people, it's okay. Some people think, no-no, shouldn't be shown, it's India. (Arun)

Despite this example, it would perhaps be more accurate to characterize the overall response of participants (while also acknowledging that this study did not validate these remarks by interviewing parents) as supporting a certain degree of normalization of images that may have once been considered obscene. This does not imply that audiences are embracing some of these new images wholeheartedly. It may simply be the case that parents find fewer cultural resources (as they had in the past) to censor such images because of their sheer pervasiveness in television—not necessarily so much in Western music videos, but in Indian film songs as well.[5] This is nicely captured in a statement by an advertising executive who says that while no one would deny the obscenity in many film songs, their presence on television conveys the idea that "someone has deemed them okay for us to watch" (quoted in Shah, 1997, p. 135).

Intergenerational negotiations of what is considered "okay to watch" are, however, only one aspect of generational issues involved in watching music television. Although it may be an exaggeration to characterize young participants as a "watching generation" and their parents and older participants as a "listening generation" in relation to music television, there are some indications that the emphasis on watching is something that is self-consciously considered a youth practice. At the outset, even the question, "Do you have a favorite music video?" evoked mixed responses. One participant, a young man in high school, said he liked an Indian pop music video, *Loveology*, because it dealt with themes young people could relate to (the video shows a nerdy young man whose eyes bulge out into animated heartshapes at passing women). Some of the participants in one of the groups that was familiar with international pop mentioned *November Rain*.

For most of the remaining participants, however, the question did not seem immediately clear, and I had to clarify it by asking if there were any songs for which they liked the visuals very much. Some of the younger participants then mentioned the names of some recent Hindi films, while one participant, a postgraduate student, said that his favorite video was a Bob Marley concert. Yet, two of the older middle-class participants mentioned two songs from early 1950s Telugu cinema. For the working-class participants, this question, like many others, did not seem meaningful.

The investment being made by music television channels in cultivating a youth audience[6] is apparent in some cases. There seems to be a perception among some participants that their generation is more interested in watching music than that of their parents. The following statement, made in the context of a discussion of Alisha's *Made in India*, indicates that Arun's parents like the song, but may not share his interest in watching the music video: "Both of them [parents] like it, but to see the video doesn't occur to them."

This statement may indicate that there are some generational differences in the normalization of watching music in general, to the extent that the soundtrack may be transgenerational, whereas the video may be more of interest to younger viewers alone. The importance of music videos to teenagers is also emphasized by another participant:

> See, I can tell about teenagers. We assume in that song that, we assume, we ourselves [are] singing that song or something like that. When we are hearing that, we cannot do that. I can say that about teenagers, we do that. I guess not all of us, but some do. (Samir)

Music television is perceived as being especially useful for teenagers, as it enables them to imagine that they are singing the song. For instance, for the participant quoted above, this is not enabled by listening to the soundtrack alone. Samir's comment illustrates the ways in which visualization in general perhaps aids in the construction of a generational identification for the emerging Indian pop music culture. The normalization of watching music television in its present stage may not necessarily take the form of an oppositional one in generational terms. However, between the eagerness of younger viewers to consume music television, the apparent absence of a broader cultural will to permit parents to regulate this, and the efforts being made particularly by Channel V and MTV India in carving out a youth market over the long term, there is no doubt that music television has established at least some of its conventions and demands for meaningful reception among audiences. The implications of this media- and market-driven youth culture may seem less ominous than they are in the light of the somewhat ambiguous and overlapping generational readings seen in this chapter. Their true relevance to questions of globalization and culture, however, may be better appreciated in relation to the reception of the countdown genre itself, and the numerous examples of music video nationalism that have appeared in Indian music television.

CHAPTER 3

LIBERALIZATION AND THE PUBLIC

By Demand,
Mangta Hai (We want),
Mee Maata Mee Paata (Your words, Your songs),
Peoples' Club,
Popularly Yours,
Public Demand,
V People . . .
—A sample of television program titles

Speak, and the rest will listen.
—Promo for Channel V's Indian Top Ten

The emancipatory connotations of the term "liberalization"—notwithstanding the actual implications it may have as economic policy—resonate in the perceptions that participants in this study seem to have about satellite television. The widespread view among middle-class participants seems to be that privatization and commercialization have made television accessible and representative. This view is embedded in the negotiation of the discourse of rankings that is seen by participants as central to the premise of the music countdown and is also strengthened by their readings of music television programs that feature on-the-street interviews with the "public."

The premise of countdowns as a genre is understood by most participants to mean reflecting public opinion and/or the merits of featured songs. However, the genre as such does not constitute an intelligible category for some of the older middle-class participants as well as the working-class participants. In this chapter, I examine how participants who recognize the premise of the genre construct preferred, negotiated, and oppositional meanings (Hall, 1973/1993) and engage with the question of value as represented in the enumerative discourse of rankings that constitute countdowns. Subsequently, I show how these readings, in conjunction with the readings of public shows as universal, realistic, and representative support an emerging sense of empowerment among audience members through television. I use the term "empowerment," however, not to celebrate audience readings of countdowns and public shows as indicating any real political gain, but as a way to understand, on the terms of the participants, how media representations and audience readings are connected to the broader field of social and political struggle in the contemporary Indian context.

At the same time, I do not wish to suggest that audiences are duped in any sense by the representations of the public that they encounter on television. As John Hartley (1992) argues, the public is in some ways a "fiction," but it is a fiction that carries investments and has consequences. In order to appreciate some of these implications, it would be useful to examine how the idea of the public is actually made meaningful in reception. Is there indeed a "need" for people who watch television to consume this fiction about themselves as the public, as John Peters (1993) suggests? This chapter explores how this need may be necessitated by the growing divide between the reality of contemporary urban public life in India and the sanitized representations of the same on television. I argue that audience investment in the notion of the public may come from a longing for community that is increasingly unavailable given the nature of social relations under economic liberalization.

Constructing Countdowns

While the preferred meaning of countdowns cannot be inferred from the genre's textual features or producers' intentions alone, the notion that countdowns are supposed to represent the public's judgment about music is a claim that producers of countdowns frequently make. For instance, Farhad Samar, the producer of *Superhit Muqabla*, launched his new countdown *Hum Aapke Hain Kountdown* (We Are Your Countdown) with the claim that "it is a countdown of the people, by the people, and for the people." Samar opines that his show is more representative than others because it is based on viewer feedback through letters, as opposed to retail sales ("Tellybuzz," 1997).

Given the lack of a universal measure of popularity for countdown producers, the accuracy of countdowns seems to be a matter of some concern in the music television business. Ken Ghosh, India's premier music video director and producer of EL TV's straightforwardly named *The Real Countdown*, goes so far as to say that music companies are often candid (if only in private) about the lack of "accuracy" in various countdowns (Naik and Karani, 1997). Some producers say that they would like to see the institution of a "proper body to govern the system" of countdowns in the absence in India of electronic systems such as Billboard's Soundscan (Naik and Karani, 1997). Some programs use well-known marketing companies for rankings research. *Superhit Muqabla* credits Dun and Bradstreet for its ratings, while *BPL Oye* follows the research of MARG. Other programs, such as *All the Best* use their own sampled measures of album sales, while other countdowns provide either in-house credits or simply give no credits at all for rankings research. In general, however, the most widespread bases for charts are based either on sales, or on viewer requests.

The apparent lack of rigorous and uniform standards has not, however, deterred the perception in the music and television businesses that countdowns are successful from the commercial perspective, not only in attracting audiences, but also in promoting music and film revenues. For instance, the producer of *Ek Se Badkar Ek* says "(countdowns) certainly make people aware of songs and decide to buy a cassette" (Naik and Karani, 1997). Music and film companies thus have a keen interest in having their products ranked high on countdowns. For the producers of countdowns, this may involve a trade-off between what their own research or judgment tells them about popularity, and having to accommodate the requests of film and music producers. As Ken Ghosh points out, while the top four songs may be consistent across different countdowns out of a real deference to the measured popularity of these songs, the ranking of songs further down the charts is open for all sorts of "favors and manipulations" (Naik and Karani, 1997).

In spite of the differences in the methods, samples, and definitions used in the construction of countdowns, the programs are quite similar to each other in their appeals to audiences as being authentic and representative. The promo for Channel V's *Indian Top Ten*, for instance, presents the program with the slogan "speak, and the rest will listen" (accompanied by images of microphones and the names of famous "speakers" such as Socrates, Einstein, and Vyasa, the quasimythical "author" of the ancient Hindu epic *The Mahabharatha*). This promo may be the best example of the preferred meaning of countdowns in India, not only for its claims to empower the audience, but also in the way that this empowerment is situated in terms of nationality in a competitive international context (a topic that will be discussed in greater detail in the following chapter).

The preferred meaning of countdowns, in terms of producers' claims and textual appeals may hence be characterized as a gesture of empowerment toward the audience. As some of the program titles quoted at the beginning of this chapter suggest, there appears to be a keen interest among television producers to present their programs as interactive and participatory. These strategies include weekly contests with attractive prizes[1] such as jewelry and cars for guessing which song would be number one the following week. One measure of the success of these interactive strategies in making countdowns popular may be seen in the fact that the Indian Postal Service was forced to issue a new kind of postcard in the early 1990s exclusively for television contest participants following a shortage of regular postcards. Despite the obvious attraction of exorbitant prizes in popularizing countdown shows, it is also worth examining how the readings of countdowns, and the sense of community they seem to offer, may also offer some explanation for their popularity.

The Meaning of Countdowns

All except working-class participants had something to say in response to the question, "What do you think is the purpose of a countdown show?" While some older middle-class participants responded with "entertainment," for the most part, participants understood the countdown genre as one that indicates public opinion and popularity. They responded that the show exists to:

> collect the demand of the public and to show which song is playing at what position. (Kamala)

> entertain the people, and to tell the people which song is hit. Top songs are like that. Many countdown shows are there, for songs, for heroines, top actresses, like that. (Pragathi)

> show us what's on top. (Pratibha)

These statements may be seen as preferred readings of the genre, and show that these participants understand the premise of countdowns. In addition, the difference between countdowns and noncountdown music television programs is also understood on the basis of the same premise, although in slightly different ways by the following participants. When asked to compare her feelings when watching a countdown and watching a noncountdown program like *Chitrahar*, one participant says:

> Each program has its own specialty, like, in *Santoor Top Ten* and all we hear the song and we can know the public demand also, public, which song they are liking most. In *Santoor Top Ten* we can make out. *So many people are liking that song, that's why it's got to come first.* Comparatively, with *Chitrahar*, such kind of thing is not seen. So, only the Doordarshan people, what they like, which [they think] is good, they'll telecast. (Kamala) (emphasis added)

Although this participant indicates that both sorts of programs may have their own merits, she perceives the representative premise of countdowns as important—not only because viewers can learn about the popularity of the songs—but more importantly, because the popularity of the songs represents a challenge to state-controlled Doordarshan. Thus, the premise of countdowns—their ability to express popularity—is considered as a live social process of empowerment rather than an abstract ideal.

The preferred reading of countdowns may thus be taken to indicate that most middle-class participants assume, through such a reading, a sense of authority for themselves through the notion that they are being represented. The notion that "so many people are liking that song," especially when contrasted with the observation that "Doordarshan people" feature only the songs they think are "good," indicates an investment in the countdown's representative claims. This participant assumes authority through such an investment because she feels that people, such as herself, have the power to influence what they see on countdowns, as opposed to the fact that only bureaucrats control Doordarshan. While other participants do not go so far in directly contrasting private channels with Doordarshan, their positions on the countdown's premise seem to implicitly support the notion that the people are indeed being represented in and through television.

Such a perception, however, does not mean that participants do not question the veracity of countdowns—although, even in the case of those who do questions the charts' claims, the premise of representativeness is itself uncontested. In contrast to the earlier statement lauding private channels in comparison to Doordarshan, one participant (who is also an avid watcher of international channels) argues that Doordarshan is in fact more representative of the people:

> *Chitrahar*, I think, as far as the rating is concerned it is much more better. Because here countdown is too commercial. Eventually it depends on who you know . . . so the song that's number one, you may not like it, but somebody who pushes from behind [will make it] number one. (Samir)

While this comment may be seen as an oppositional reading, because it rejects the specific claims of countdowns to represent the public, it is interesting that certain attributes of countdowns are invoked even in the discussion of a noncountdown show like *Chitrahar*, suggesting that the premise of representativeness remains intact. *Chitrahar*, which was used a counterexample to countdowns in the interviews, is also seen as representing public taste through its "rating." This participant thus believes that the public is represented more openly in *Chitrahar* than in countdowns, as these are, according to him, commercial and perhaps dishonest. However, it is important that the concept of representativeness remains the basis of his position, and as he goes on to say:

> I think *Chitrahar* is better than any other program because it is by the people. The nature of the Indians is most often shown on this *Chitrahar* or some other shows like that. *Chitralahari* and many of those shows. Because they give the songs, which are given [requested] in the letters they get, the letters they get from the people, they play those songs. So, it's by the people, I can say, from the people. (Samir)

While such a strong statement of support for the representativeness of *Chitrahar* or Doordarshan is not made by any other participant, there are further instances of readings in which the countdown's integrity, in terms of its premise of representativeness, is questioned. One more participant is critical of countdowns for their commercial function and contrasts this with their implicit claims to representativeness:

> It is a marketing strategy for the music people liking the songs . . . because everyone claims that they are showing the countdown on [the basis of] making the survey, the survey of the public. Then how come they differ in all the countdowns? Songs are always different in all the countdowns. Except for two [or] three songs maybe. The thing is that (emphatically). (Arun)

In addition, the participant who prefers *Chitrahar* also says elsewhere:

> Those people [countdown producers], they are money-minded. And they are seeing what the popular countdown is from the theaters, where they get the ratings and all. (Samir)

While the statements of these viewers indicate slightly different sorts of oppositional readings of countdowns, it is significant that they are the only statements that question the ability of commercial interests to represent the public. It does not necessarily imply that other participants are ignorant about the commercial interests underlying countdowns, but they certainly prefer to talk about the opportunities for representation that countdowns offer rather than any possible dilution of the same by their commercial imperative. In the following example, the participant does not necessarily perceive a contradiction between the commercial basis of countdowns and their representative premise:

> They all say it's on the basis of sales and more or less it is in the same order, but here and there there are differences, what is number one [in one chart] may not be number one on another chart. (Anila)

This statement indicates a negotiated reading of countdowns in that the participant notices discrepancies in the specific ranks that songs are assigned in various countdowns, but at the same time she is only holding countdown producers to their own claims of basing their charts on sales and not necessarily challenging the ability of sales to reflect popularity. In the preferred, negotiated, and oppositional readings described above, the purpose of countdowns is therefore fairly plainly understood by viewers. There is also an investment made by viewers in the premise of representativeness to the extent that this is applied in different contexts, such as assessing *Chitrahar*, and in evaluating the instrumental veracity of the countdown's claims.

The premise of representativeness of countdowns may be constructed by viewers from their engagement not only with specific countdowns, but with promos, fillers, and other top ten charts that are now widely circulated in newspapers and magazines as well. At the same time, the countdown as a genre carries one central feature that is essential to its claims; namely, the chart, with its songs featured in a ranked order. The ranking of songs is highlighted within the programs through the usual climactic fervor that is generated in reaching the "number one" song for the week (with prizes for guessing) and in the prominent display of graphics that highlight each song's rank and its relative position in comparison to the previous week.

From a commercial perspective, ranking is seen as vital to an album or film's success, but participants respond to the discourse of ranking with varying degrees of attention, interest, and investment. On the specific issue of music sales, some participants indicate that they had on occasion purchased an album because of its high ranking on the charts, while for the most part they say that they had bought popular albums not necessarily because they were number one, but because they liked what they saw and heard.

The discourse of rankings is central to the ways in which viewers construct not only meanings of popularity and representativeness around the countdown genre, but also in the ways in which viewers experience the flow of countdown programs. While working-class participants either do not know or only wager a guess about what the numbers that precede songs may mean, most of the other participants engage with rankings in some form or the another. For instance, with regard to the question, "Do you pay attention to the rank of a song?" many responses were positive, as the following example indicates:

> Yeah. We definitely see whether, which position it [a song] is. Because, see, last week it was in second position. We would like to know which position it is in this week. (Kamala)

Like this participant, others say that they are interested in knowing the progress of a song from week to week, but are often confounded by the fact that the same song may have different ranks on different countdowns:

> Everybody keeps counting [on] other countdowns. So there's no particular concentration about what countdown we can remember the top one from, and say [which is] the top one in another one. (Arun)

The profusion of countdowns, however, and the speed with which songs are shown on them, also causes some problems in noticing the rank of songs, for another participant. She feels, however, that being able to watch the same program more than once (most countdowns are rerun at least twice during the course of the week) allows her to remember the specific ranks of songs:

> Of course [I pay attention to ranking] . . . but not [if the song is seen] only once, [but if it is seen] twice or thrice. If we'll see the . . . means . . . it's somewhat fast, so if we see twice or thrice means, okay, you can judge the thing. (Pragathi)

Although repeated viewing may reinforce viewer attention and recall of the rank of specific songs, it would not be accurate to overstate the importance of ranking as if it is valuable information that viewers retain all the time. As the following participant says:

> It can be enjoyed just as long as you watch it. Then there is no thinking about it again. It's only as long as you're watching it, then you forget about it. (Raja) (translated from Telugu)

At the same time, this participant feels that the rankings in a sense do matter during the course of the program; not necessarily in their application to specific songs, but as a way in which some kind of an order is set up for the songs, culminating in songs from the new films, which he finds most appealing:

> In those rankings, some stars' films are in, and some stars' films are out. If you see one star's song in the beginning, you know there will be another star's song in the end, a hit cinema, right? Everyone sits and waits for the hit cinema. Everyone, just for that. That's how it works. Whether you're watching number six or number seven, your interest is just for songs from the new films alone. (Raja) (translated from Telugu)

Another participant agrees with this assessment of the role of rankings in structuring the program and creating suspense, but distances himself from such an experience. According to him, the lyrics of the title song of *Superhit Muqabla* exhort viewers to take an interest, but it does not mean that viewers necessarily do take such an active interest:

> They are basically trying to get us interested. In knowing who is the top three. Basically, it is something we are not interested in knowing. Like [quoting from the lyrics] *'hafta-hafta rasta-rasta koun hain number one?'* [Who's number one week after week?] (Arun)

The main implication of rankings for participants, however, pertains not so much to the suspense (or lack thereof) in the program, but to the fact that they represent a certain degree of value for songs they like, as I discuss below in relation to Simon Frith's (1996) work. While it may not be the case that participants would like a song only because of its high rank on the charts, there are numerous instances of the opposite being true. Participants clearly pay attention to the rank that is assigned to songs they like, often with some degree of investment in whether the rank is a fair indicator of what they think the song deserves:

> It so happens that you notice your favorite songs, whether it's come down or come up. Others, you don't see twice. We don't pay much attention to other songs. (Bhanu)

> Sometimes I wonder why a song I liked isn't on the top. (Pratibha)

> Sometimes, you know, they are better than the second ones, but they are thrown to fourth or fifth, then we'll feel bad. [We feel] how come this decision was taken? (Kamala)

These comments indicate a sense of personal investment in the ranking of songs, but at the same time, these are also related to the underlying notion of public taste. Most participants do not make a distinction between their own taste and that of the public, which the rankings are taken to represent. Thus, these participants talk about the ranking of the songs as an indicator of both:

> Top ten means any song which has become popular because it should [deserves to] become popular. (Anjali)

> I personally feel [the purpose of a countdown] is to assess the music and the way of taking the song, all these things. Especially the music part. The director, how he has composed the song, like that. To assess that, mostly to attract the audience too. That's my assessment. (Murali)

The above comments suggest that the songs on a countdown earn their place not only because of their innate merits, but also because these merits would earn them the support of the public. The rankings are seen, like countdowns in general, as indicating what the public seems to think is the best. On the one hand, for participants who are familiar with a wide range of countdowns (including international ones), this notion becomes easy to sustain, given the fact that international countdowns are supposed to represent different publics as opposed to the Hindi film music ones:

> Pratibha: [Rankings are similar] probably for Hindi countdown. Not English countdown. On MTV it's different . . . their [U. S.] music is totally different. I don't like it.
>
> Anila: Too techno.
>
> Sonia: They like techno. U. S. is something else. Asian [top 20] is something else. Indian now is something else.

While this exchange illustrates a perception that ranking may be more reliable for foreign countdowns (given that the context of these remarks was the confusion caused by the multiple rankings of Hindi countdowns), these participants are also clear in distancing themselves from the kind of music they associate with Western countdowns. Although these participants are among the few in this study with the greatest degree of familiarity with MTV and Channel V, they do not identify with the kind of public that may be underlying the Western countdowns on the basis of taste. A similar situation is described by some participants in the case of Hindi countdowns as well, although, on this occasion, the problem is not the music but the fact that there are simply many Hindi countdowns with their own ranking sequence; sometimes, as noted in the following example, on the same channel:

> I noticed that *Superhit Muqabla* has a number one and it isn't so for *All the Best. All the Best* moves differently and this moves differently. (Radhika)

While this participant does not speculate on the possible reasons for these differences, there is an implication that these programs are either not representative, or that there may be different kinds of publics involved in the two programs. The fact that there may be different ranks for the same songs, or even the fact that some songs may not deserve the ranks that they get, however, is addressed by another participant's comment. Her perception seems to be that her own tastes would not matter so much, because it is the "public" that has to come first:

> We have to take the public first. Because anyway they are going to see that program. They are sponsoring for the public only. They have to take their, which song they are demanding, like that. (Jyothi)

In spite of the differences claimed from the public on occasion, the more pervasive trend among participants seems to be that their own tastes are not very different from that of the public. The key point here, however, is that the meaningful reconstitution of the premise of countdowns by some participants may indicate a naturalization of rankings as a way of presenting music and popularity. The following exchange, on whether viewers need to know the rank of a song, illustrates this point:

> Anila: I do need to know [what the rankings are].
>
> Deepika: Why do you need to know? I mean it isn't like, if you just have to, why do you have to rank it? If you just have top ten, if you just have ten, and you say these are the ten best ones for this month, without making each one of them the best.

While one participant's "need to know" rankings is challenged by her friend, the alternative proposed by her does not escape the premise of representativeness, either. Thus, although she feels that she can do without having songs ranked in a particular order, at the same time she is compelled to propose instead that the "ten best ones for the month" are what should be featured in the first place. The notion of the "best ones" draws attention to the question of value, whether in terms of pleasure, or in terms of popularity.

Such value judgments made by people in their everyday lives, as Frith (1996) argues, are central to how music and popular culture become meaningful. According to Frith, these value judgments are not merely expressed in the form of personal or subjective declarations such as "I like/you like," but are instead rooted in a firm belief in the objective nature of the qualities being debated. At the same time, even as a sense of objectiveness is invoked by those who are engaged in such talk about popular culture, there is also a sense of subjectivity involved, especially given the fact that those who may hold certain ideas as objective evaluations may be seen by others as being certain kinds of people *because* of their belief in such ideas. Talking about popular culture thus may be seen as playing a crucial role in the construction of notions of identity and reality by participants.

Frith's observations are relevant to this study because music television—especially the countdown with its discourse of ranking—may be seen as a way of assigning value to popular culture, indicating that viewers negotiate in their everyday lives not only the value of music, but also the value assigned to music on television. Although, as Frith points out, a "measurement of popularity . . . is not a measurement of value" (p. 48), the perception of rankings among participants as described above indicates that rankings are seen as an assessment of both. Participants seem to feel that a countdown song has value broadly on the basis of its innate merits, and also on the basis of the translation of those merits into popular taste (although, at times popular taste is also invoked as something that is not capable of appreciating quality).

While the criteria that participants use to judge the innate merits of a song may not be relevant to this study, there is no doubt that "popularity" figures as a significant notion in the reception of music countdowns. However, if the popular is defined, as Frith argues, as the "cultural sector in which all participants claim the authority to pass judgment" (p. 9), it is also possible that the countdown may not constitute popularity in a rigorous sense if the class differences encountered in this study are any indication. Working-class participants watch film music programs on television too, but the discourses of music television in general are outside their zone of intelligibility, at least to the extent revealed in this study.

These differences may be situated in the context of the class-based distribution of access to various forms of mass-mediated cultures in contemporary India, particularly the intersections of film and television cultures which are highlighted by the countdown genre. Although music television may be a form of "mass culture" rather than "high culture," mass culture, as Frith (1996) points out, cannot be simply equated with working-class culture. Mass culture has often been middle-class culture, according to Frith, a fact that is true in the Indian context as well.

What is perhaps unique to the Indian context, however, is the fact that high culture in India may be located not only in the Indian classical traditions, but also in the fact that until recently (and perhaps even to this day) Western mass culture was by no means accessible to the masses, and becomes, by default, a form of high culture in the Indian context. Another development that is significant to the Indian context is the change in the audience for Indian cinema. While Indian cinema has traditionally been aimed at working-class audiences, the rise of music television has also served to make Indian cinema "cool" for young, middle-class music television audiences.[2]

Cinema, by virtue of its appeal to working-class audiences, may represent a true "popular" medium in India, while music countdowns, with their largely middle-class audiences invested in the premise of popular representation, represent "popularity." However, this popularity is neither defined nor perceived solely in terms of sales, but may be seen as a way in which audience members assign value to popular culture as well. Therefore, it may be argued that countdowns represent an organized practice for the assignment of value to music, not only on the basis of sales and popularity, but more importantly in the ways in which viewers negotiate the countdowns themselves.

While the preponderance of numbers and enumeration in countdowns may not necessarily be accurate representations given the admittedly loose methods of polling used by producers, what is indeed important—as shown by some of the statements made above—is that the numbers may not literally stand for value in terms of popularity, but are seen instead as a way of making a legitimate claim about the value of a song. Thus, the numbers that are assigned to songs in the countdown may not always be taken literally by participants but at the same time the process of assigning numbers is seen in general as a way of assigning value to songs. For instance, in response to a question regarding what "number one" means in the context of music countdowns, one participant says:

> Number ones are *Dilwale Dulhaniya Le Jayinge*. Before that, *Hum Aapke Hain Koun*. (Uday)

It is significant that "number one" isn't described by him as "the most popular or best-selling album of that week"—although he may know that this is what it means by definition. Instead, he associates the notion of being "number one" with the music from two popular Hindi films. While these films may have indeed been "number one" in terms of their box-office records and music sales, this may not be the only implication of the term. In other words, "number one" may be even be a nonliteral way of suggesting that something represents value, whether in terms of its musical features or in terms of its popularity. For instance, the term is also used frequently by working-class participants in various public shows, without referring to any underlying basis for that claim. Finally, the phrase "number one" has become so widespread in and around music television that MTV features a promo ("simply number one") that puns on the phrase's body-function connotation using a dog, a wall with religious icons, and a very Indian situation in general.

Popular Voices

The implications of these readings for the broader social processes of liberalization in India rests in the fact that a song being "number one" is arguably understood by participants as a sign of recognition on the part of television programmers and producers of their authority as part of the public to bestow such a value for the song, presumably on the basis of the public's ability to recognize the song's merits. Such a perception is also evident in the statements made by some participants to the effect that television *in general* has become more accessible to the public because of private satellite channels. These perceptions also seem to derive from a growing awareness among participants of their location in an "imagined community" in precisely the sense that Anderson (1991) uses the term—often in relation to specific textual features in music television programs.

Increasingly, it appears that the value of television programs is seen by viewers as being dependent upon its viewers. In other words, as the following remark indicates, the message of the title song of *Superhit Muqabla* is seen by one participant as suggesting that the program promises not only entertainment for viewers, but also the promise of identification with other distinguished viewers as well:

> Lyrics are intelligent. They try to tell us *Superhit Muqabla* is the best show. If you are the [type of] people . . . [who watch] any of the best shows, you better watch it, kind of. (Arun)

The title song, according to this participant, tells the viewer that if you (the viewer) are the kind of person who watches the best shows, then you better watch this one. While it is unclear what specific textual configurations enable the viewer to make this particular meaning, it indicates that at least some viewers see certain forms of contemporary televisual address as hailing them selfconsciously as viewers of that show. A similar perception is also evident in the following remark:

> [MTV is for those who] want the right song and right VJs to be there, it's for that kind of people only. (Maya)

These remarks, it may be argued, support an emerging form of selfconsciousness among audience members that ties into notions of distinction and superiority. The remark about MTV in particular suggests that viewers see the overall role of MTV as one in which it offers itself only to those who know what is "right"—in terms of songs, VJs, jokes, fashions, and so on. The message of television, in different contexts, is taken to suggest that viewers may derive their own value as cool viewers from watching a cool program or channel, which in turn is cool because it is being watched by all the cool people.

However, in the context of this study, it appears that the emerging self-consciousness of some participants as audience members does not express itself so much as an overt form of cultural superiority, but appears to sustain, quite contradictorily, the opposite—an egalitarian, universal sensibility about the public. In other words, neither the two participants above nor any other participants make any explicit claims to insider knowledge on MTV or about being "cool" in general; notwithstanding the larger culture of one-upmanship and conspicuous consumption that liberalization entails. For one thing, the above comments suggest neither an endorsement of such a message, nor do they represent resistance to such a message.

In the context of the larger sensibilities that participants seem to inhabit in relation to the notions of the public, it would appear that the emerging self-consciousness among audiences *as* audiences, or as the public, is seen primarily as something that may be enabled by television channels that are more open to them, but definitely not as a co-optation by television. In other words, the selfconsciousness that audience members feel in relation to television is not restricted to television; they appear to perceive themselves as primarily the public, a community that television is now beginning to represent.

The representation of the public as a community clearly overlaps both the public and private in the kind of questions that participants in public shows are frequently asked. These questions may pertain to issues that are often considered a part of the private sphere, such as questions on relationships, family, children, and so on. Public shows, in addition, represent—at least on the surface—the everyday world of middle-class Indians, which includes a constant interaction with less-privileged Indians as well. To some extent, public shows may show life as it seems to happen, but without the tempers and ugly scenes, either between members of the lumpen elite classes, or more importantly, between middle- and working-class members in the latter's pervasive displays of what Sudipta Kaviraj (1998) calls "rising insubordination" in his discussion of public culture in contemporary urban India (p. 169).

Real TV

While I will return shortly to the social tensions that these shows ignore, it must be noted that participants for the most part like these shows (this was apparent not only from their statements but also from how some of them reacted excitedly to the clip from *Public Demand* during the interviews). One term that participants frequently use to describe these shows is "real"—and it must be emphasized that they mean "real," and not "realistic." In other words, public shows are not seen as a staged act of representation that strives to faithfully represent reality, but as a rather simple and unmediated picture of reality itself. The following statements indicate some of the ways in which this sensibility emerges:

> I think it's *[Public Demand]* the best countdown . . . it's the real public. They go out onto the road and talk to people. (Alpana)

> They interview every person, on the roads. (Ajay)

> The natural scenes, they take on roads, and all the sights. (Pragathi)

The notion of reality, as indicated in these statements, comes out of the location of these shows, as well as the fact that participants in the shows are not professional performers. The location of these shows is perhaps central to the experience of their being seen as real, because of the fact that these are places that people who watch TV could very well be in (the regional language channels certainly film a lot of their public shows in small towns in the "interior" of the state as well). For the most part, these are on streets, public spaces like parks, in shops, and in shopping complexes. In addition, a number of programs on local cable channels also feature variations on public shows. These are not so much music-based, but are simply home video-style recordings of local community events and festivals. However, it is not only the location of these shows, but what participants say and do—often with all their undisguised imperfections and seeming ignorance—on these shows that make them real:

> [I like it because] the fact comes out. The way sometimes they show that, the, countdown through the scenes. Sometimes they're just shooting interviews, they don't know what's going on in the music world. Most of them, *ye picture mein hero kaun tha*? [who was the hero in this picture?] They think Urmila is same as Madhuri Dixit, something like that. The reality comes out. Whether it is really hit or they are making it hit. So such shows are good and then they're playing what the public wanted. . . . Most of the time, *bekaar gaana hai to bi dekhlenge, bakwas karre* [even if it's a bad song we'll watch it, because they're talking nonsense]. (Arun)

This participant sees public shows as doubly real; he is able to ascertain the veracity of the countdown's claims ("whether it is hit or they are making it hit") through the presence of the people who are speaking, and also find amusement in the fact that some of these people may not be well informed about music or movies and mistake one actress for another (apparent in the statement "they think Urmila is same as Madhuri Dixit"). In addition, the things that people say on these shows are characterized by him as not just a form of entertainment, but a veritable attraction that gets one "stuck" to the TV, even if the songs are not especially enjoyable. The performance of participants on these shows is hence seen as a source of pleasure, sometimes at their expense.

> Actually, that's what they get to see, the foolishness, the craziness of getting on TV. *Kuch bi bolenge, abbe* [they'll say anything, hey], I'll be on TV types. I should say something prominent. You get to see all this foolishness. We can have a laugh on that. (Arun)

While the "craziness" of what people on public shows say is a source of entertainment for this viewer, it also makes some participants wary in believing what they say, or even disgusted with the whole genre:

> I don't know if they mean what they say, it's just the excitement of getting on TV. (Radhika)

> Sometimes they ask such stupid questions. All the people answer with stupid answers. It's like you just can't stand all the rubbish going on on TV. I'd rather not watch the songs also that come over there. Too much. (Padma)

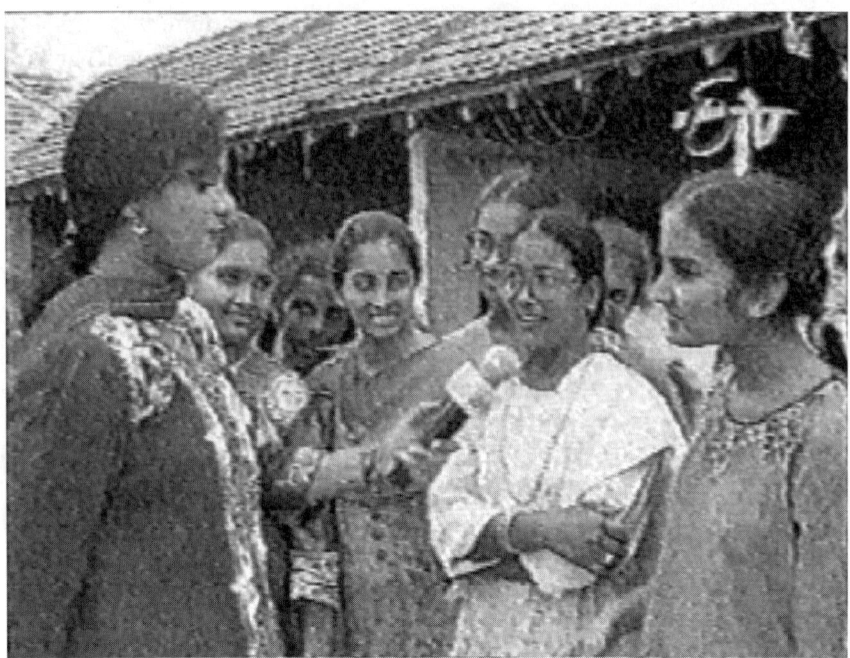

FIGURE 4 Hrudayanjali in the heartland. The Telugu language channel ETV's public show features participants from small towns and villages. In this segment, the VJ is asking them what they talk about when they walk to college.

Thus, not all participants find the antics of some of the people who appear on public shows acceptable. While the above participant expresses her distaste for the programs as well as the songs that are featured, another participant, an older middle-class professional who is in general not invested in the various genre conventions of countdowns, says that he dislikes the whole "concept" of public shows. However, two of the working-class participants, both of whom are mothers and not a part of the countdown discourse, find public shows (at least the clip in the interview, as "public shows" again does not constitute a coherent genre for them) funny in a parentally indulgent sort of way; as one of them puts it, "The people on such shows are mostly young, and whatever young people do is funny."

In spite of the perceived excesses in the behavior of people on public shows, these shows are seen by participants as more enjoyable than many others simply due to the fact that there is a variety of voices presented on them as opposed to the single one of the VJ in other shows. In fact, the same participant who elsewhere in the interview expresses disgust with these programs, goes on to say:

> It's better, you're at least seeing so many people talking something, instead of listening to one guy talking all the nonsense that he wants to. Okay, so there are at least people, okay, you can have a good time knowing from people around you that you are not so dumb. (Deepa).

This participant may not fully endorse public shows, but also finds it reassuring that viewers can remind themselves that they are not as "dumb" as some of the people in the shows. Although this statement indicates that she is more interested in distancing herself from the sort of antics that she sees on these shows, other participants find the shows more useful and entertaining. Specifically, as the following comments indicate, public shows are simultaneously seen as representing them, and also enabling them to participate, identify, and evaluate themselves in a social context:

> We can answer the questions that they ask us. Whatever they may be showing us, they are showing it after learning about our mentality. (Gopal) (translated from Telugu)

> They put you on a scale to measure yourself, where you stand . . . *manam ikkadunnamu!* [We are here!] (Vijay)

The interactive, participatory format of these programs is seen as a way of getting personally involved in the program by evaluating oneself in relation to others, as the above comment suggests. At the same time, there is also a perception that public shows represent a larger democratization of television not only in terms of what people say, but also in terms of what songs people get to choose, supporting the readings of countdowns and rankings discussed earlier.

"Power to the Public"

It is significant that the opportunity that public shows provide for evaluating oneself in relation to others is not seen as a merely recreational exercise, but as an empowering process. Thus, as the following participant says:

> The aim of the program is just a quiz. It makes you feel like at least okay, there are lots of people who write in for shows, contests or whatever, and they'll choose the countdown. They actually feel that they are, because we wanted it, that has come. Public gives them that idea. It's very social, the public demand. In fact, the power to the public, that's what it makes them feel. (Radhika)

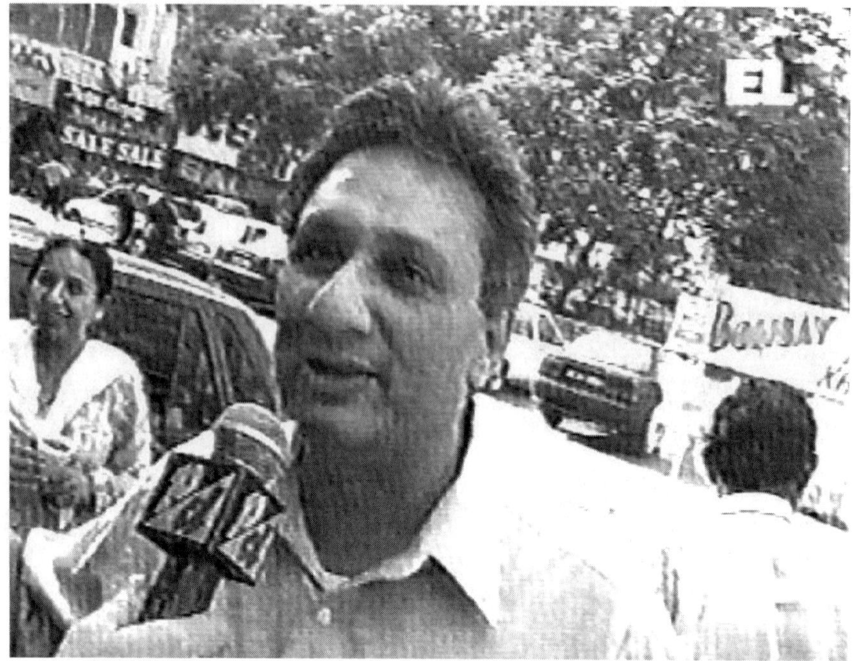

FIGURE 5 Q: "What is the best way to reach God?" A: "By Concorde." From El TV's countdown Public Demand.

A similar feeling of being recognized by television, of feeling that "because we wanted it that has come," is also evident in the following statements, which situate such a feeling more directly in the immediate context of the present, which includes both liberalization and the rise of private satellite television channels:

> Nowadays there's more focus on peoples' opinions, they try to collect the people's feelings about a program or about life. Earlier it wasn't like that. (Bhanu)

> Before this ETV songs no, when Doordarshan used to produce those kind of programs, we used to feel the distance of Doordarshan,[3] somewhere there, [while we were] sitting at home only. [When new shows] like this *Hrudayanjali* come, we feel that we are able to see songs [and] we can tell our ideas, suggestions, and our views [which] can be shown on the screen. So, something, that nearness has come now. That awareness has come to everybody in the city, we can say, or in the village, for now everybody talks on TV programs and all. Before this that was very limited. And we used to feel the distance is always there. Now we feel we can approach ETV people or Gemini people. (Kamala)

Public shows, countdowns, and by extension satellite television in general are seen quite emphatically as being more accessible to participants and people in general as opposed to Doordarshan. For the participant who feels that she can now approach ETV and Gemini, it is not only as a participant in a public show, but also as a performer. The private channels thus represent greater opportunity for her than Doordarshan could possibly provide. For the other participants however, access in terms of being a part of the public is not seen as a fundamental problem, and the only criterion for being on a public show according to them is simply being there:

> Anybody who walks on the road and they'll cut you in. (Pratibha)

> We sometimes feel like why is Roshan Abbas not in front of me, we could have also answered. (Vijay)

> It's not like they just get these people together to be a part of it. (Anila)

As these comments illustrate, participants see themselves as part of the public and that the only criterion[4] to be on a public show is to be there at the right time and place (although one participant problematized the fact that as the crew couldn't ask the hundreds of people walking on the street, they would settle for those who, according to one participant, "looked kind of different or like the kind who watched TV.") The perceived universality of the public is hence not without its nuances, although participants clearly do not express a perception that access to being a part of the public may be stratified on the basis of class.

Everyone and Everybody

Class differences, a striking reality of Indian everyday life, are apparent in public shows. As described earlier, there are two main ways in which working-class people are featured in shows like *Public Demand*. Sometimes they may literally rub shoulders with everyone else, either as bystanders or as participants. At other times, they are used as fillers, often doing or saying something ridiculous. Although most middle-class participants in the study once again seemed to assume that the public included everyone, they were asked to choose during the interviews from the characters who appear in the clip shown during the interviews the people who best reflected the public; specifically, whether it would be one of the middle-class people who speak in the clip, or one of the working-class people who appear as fillers (they are not interviewed, but are a standard feature used in the program to signal the rank of a song).

In response, at least one participant unequivocally answers that they would all be a part of the public:

> Everybody would be part [of the public]. Everybody would identify with something like that right from the *paanwala* to the person in the Cielo [a luxury car] they talked to. (Deepika)

However, when pressed to evaluate the role of the people who appear as fillers, participants did not have a ready answer, but instead attempted to make sense of something they may not have thought about in such a context:

> Maya: He's just to show the number of the song.
>
> Nisha: He's just asked to say [the name of the show], might be.
>
> Mamatha: I think it's some sort of entertainment thing.
>
> Nisha: Sort of, they thought, maybe some unique thing.
>
> Mamatha: It's kind of funny but, it's kind of a bad joke because there are few millions of people who watch TV, but I don't think all those millions of people watching can see such a person chewing *paan* and saying "*Public Demand*." Generally we don't get to see people doing such things.

The last statement summarizes a problem not widely identified by other participants; namely, the ethics of deriving humor (which she admittedly does as well), from the staged performances of people who may not even have access to television. While the propriety of these representations is questioned by this participant, it is not seen as a problem by another participant, because ultimately:

> They [the working-class people on public shows] just want to be known. Popular, that's it. He gets a sort of VIP treatment in the public and I think that's the reason [they participate]. (Nisha)

However, in spite of the enthusiasm with which working-class people are seen as participating in such programs, and the enthusiasm of the middle-class participants of this study in embracing them as part of the public, there are also doubts about what exactly a working-class person's class position would entail in terms of access and privilege:

Anila: The *chaiwala* [tea-seller] is also part of the same thing [public], you could be standing next to that *chaiwala* and he [the VJ] could ask you and he could ask him.

Vamsee: You think the *chaiwala* would also be watching this show?

Pratibha: Yeah.

Alpana: I have my doubts. Like if you just walk and someone has a TV [only then could he watch it, as a passerby].

Anila: I don't think so. Everybody cannot afford cable, if he has a television, that is.

Pratibha: But everybody's aware of the songs and all. The *paanwala* . . .

Deepika: But *paanwalas* are one of the very well off communities.

Alpana: The one . . .

Deepika: The one anywhere.

Alpana: Next to Hi-King or Nan-King [local Chinese restaurants].

Sonia: Next to Nan-King or anywhere.

Deepika: They're one of the most well-off communities.

While this explanation allows viewers to feel that *paanwalas* belong to a different class background, they are not necessarily disadvantaged. The urban middle-class myth about *paanwalas* being "one of the most well-off communities" may allow this explanation. Class differences are also addressed in the following statement by another participant, but in language that suggests difficulty in naming these differences as class:

> Probably even a person of that kind [would be a part of the public]. Probably many of them who are that kind you know, no, not really that kind with a scarf [referring to a poseur-type working class man in the clip with bandana and dark glasses], but that kind of mentality, and they really feel like I can also appear. It makes him feel good that he is in a channel where everything is so hi-fi. (Radhika)

This participant invokes "mentality" not necessarily in a condescending way but rather as an attempt to avoid being classist or elitist. In addition, the phenomenon of working-class people on these shows is perceived as a liberal, democratic one, where even people without "culture" in the sense of educated middle-class sensibilities may find access to appear on "hi-fi" channels. While the above responses suggest different ways in which middle-class participants try to accommodate the reality of class differences in their perception of the public, one participant sees bringing up class differences as being in poor taste:

> Everyone is good in their own way. We should not say like that. (Pragathi)

For this participant, the most appropriate response to dealing with the question of class differences is to deferentially avoid talking about it, as speaking about it would imply a presumption of superiority. A similar perception equating class and culture is made by another participant, who does not have a problem in talking about it, but on the contrary, asserts that there is no problem in watching such shows because of the presence of working-class people:

> Everybody can watch this show. It's not like if I watch this show I'm undignified. (Arun)

Once again, this participant makes an assumption that the value of television and its audiences are interdependent, this time in terms of what is considered respectable or dignified in terms of class. His remark also underscores a similar liberal democratic ideal seen in some of the comments described above in that he does not feel that watching working-class members on such shows demeans him in any way. The flip side to his remark, of course, is the implication that what people on public shows do may indeed lack dignity. The main issue, however, is not so much whether the behavior of working-class people on public shows is considered inappropriate (similar or worse kinds of inappropriate behavior are frequently in evidence from middle class participants in public shows as well), but the fact that the presence of class differences is normalized through the tacit consumption of such shows and through the espousal of liberal democratic ideals by middle-class participants in relation to these shows.

The People and the Club: Social Relations under Liberalization

Public shows may hence be seen as a discourse in which differences in privilege are normalized through invocations of notions of universality and equality. The experience of privilege by participants is of course by no means uniform and unproblematic, as everyday life is indeed not easy for most middle-class Indians. However, what is relevant is the fact that television discourses featuring working-class people as parts of Indian everyday life in an exoticized and funny sense go hand in hand with emerging ideologies of liberalization, such as competition, individualism, and meritocracy which are all staged within the noble sentiments of the notion of the public.

On this note, liberalization, with its rampant consumerism, may be seen principally as a process in which a particular commonsensical middle-class Indian notion of privilege and accountability for privilege are transformed into an ideal of prosperity for all under the auspices of private enterprise. As Sudipta Kaviraj (1998) writes, such notions have undergone dramatic changes in recent years, from a traditional sense of austerity as well as the modesty in privilege encouraged under the Nehruvian project:

> Till the 1960s, this [discretion in the enjoyment of privilege] was in part due to the traditional culture of conspicuous frugality of the merchant castes. The rise of more serious and widespread capitalist enterprise made this culture increasingly untenable, by adding to the list of the commercially wealthy entirely new groups of people untrained in the traditional caste practices of restraint. Traditional business families went by these rules until their sons returned with quite other ideas from shallow training in American business schools. . . . From the late 1970s, a new middle class introduced into the society a culture of consumer competitiveness . . . [in which] the enjoyment of pleasure or affluence lies precisely in the spectacle and the enjoyment of its denial to others. (pp. 162–3)

While Kaviraj provides a scathing summary of the historical transformation of privilege and accountability in post-independence India, it must be noted that the participants in this study, like many middle-class Indians, may not necessarily support such rampant greed and consumerism. However, it is not so much the shameless display of consumption in itself that is the issue here (although that is certainly in evidence in postliberalization India), but the fact that the enormity of the reality of class differences in India is in some ways downplayed by the celebration of a universal ideal of the public on television.

Thus, liberalization is perceived not as a process in which there is a simultaneous withdrawal of state support for underprivileged classes and a concomitant loss of a sense of accountability among the privileged classes, but rather as an indication that the world—according to television—is getting more liberal, open, and wonderful. Indeed, some privileges, such as being on television, are no longer restricted to politicians, government officials, and film stars and celebrities. Anyone, even a cobbler or a barber, can now be on television. Becoming liberal, for the middle classes, thus seems to mean that they should accept the presence of working-class people on television. They do this with no problem, and with a stout sense of faith in democracy.

However, a brief characterization of the "reality" of urban everyday life would be useful in underscoring the vast differences in what everyday life

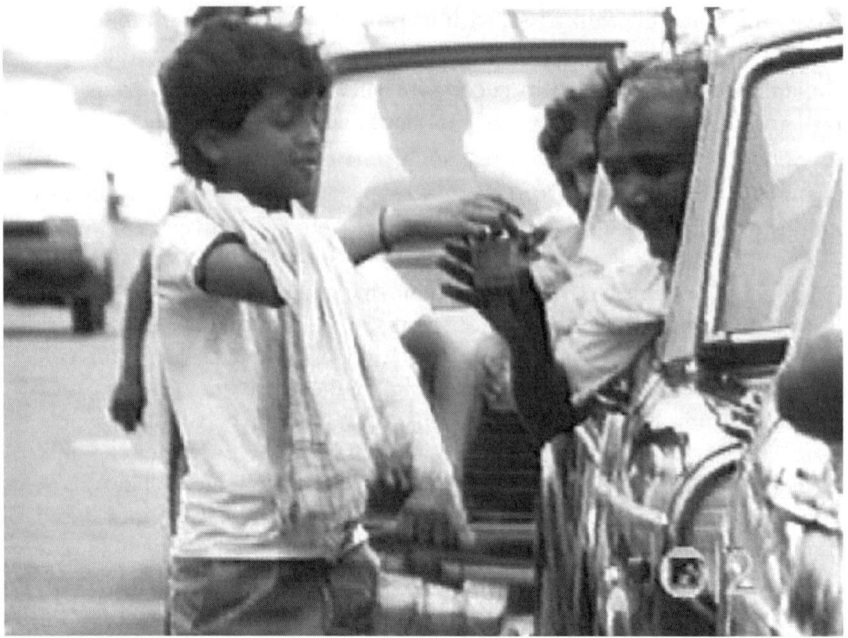

FIGURE 6 A young tea-seller in an MTV promo (shown here on MTV 2 in the United States).

entails, in contrast to the bonhomie and good spirit in which people of all classes appear in a public show. Even a few minutes waiting at a traffic intersection in an Indian city would show a veritable cross-section of society; although the most privileged are not seen, as they are in air-conditioned cars with tinted windows. The next level of privilege may be seen in those people with cars that have no air-conditioning (which means that windows are often rolled down leaving them more vulnerable than the car owners with air-conditioning).

Vehicles have their own hierarchy, with mini jeeps and some cars carrying greater "elbowing power" than others. Then, there are the three-wheeler auto-rickshaws[5] (and their idiomatic way of driving); the motorized two wheelers, consisting of middle class professionals, privileged students, and professionalized working-class people; bicycles, vending cart pushers, and pedestrians. Pedestrians include construction laborers, many of whom ride in on morning trains from villages in search of work and wait outside railway stations; beggars, who approach the people in the cars, and children hawking flags and on at least one occasion, Arundhati Roy's *The God of Small Things*.

In addition to the strong class differences evident in the space of the city, there is the increasing anonymity of everyday life. While class hostilities are clearly apparent at moments of conflict, there is sometimes an increasing need to maintain indifference and a lack of eye contact in order to avoid unpleasant situations. In contrast to this experience of the city (which is somewhat exaggerated in this account by ignoring familiarity and routine), the experience of the public in the relative comfort of one's living room affords a different experience. This is not in the least because of the cordiality with which people participate in these programs. Thus, the experience of reality may not be one that is claimed in contrast to the staged nature of TV programs in general, but also as a way of imposing meaning on the vast crowding of everyday life in the real world.

The rise of the public on television may be a part of the spectacularization of audiences in India, as Appadurai and Breckenridge (1996) claim. Thus, middle-class audiences may find it easier to consume the image of the crowd in the comfort of their homes than actually be among them. However, the public is also a representation, hitherto widely unavailable, of the reality of Indian everyday life presented in a selective, fragmented, and heightened fashion for consumption in comfortable domestic environments. The reality of this life, of course, straddles the public and the private in complex and overlapping ways, and what is at stake really at the heart of it is the question not only of the social distribution of privileges and costs under liberalization, but also of a change in the ways of understanding these.

The title of the film program *People's Club* highlights this contradiction succinctly; postliberalization television promises to the "people" the exclusivity and privilege of the "club." In reality, the club—such as the famous "Bombay Club" which has become a literal symbol of postliberalization power—is the increasingly dominant source of power in a society undergoing rapid privatization. Privatization represents not only the "retreat of the state" but also an actual retreat of power from public accountability, as seen, for instance, in the institution of the multinational corporation which is not responsible to the public in any sort of way other than through its own limited imaginings of the public as a market or a repository of consumer choice and purchasing power.

What this means in the context of the real world of the public or what people face in their daily lives is that there is little systemic accountability that exists in the relationships between classes except for the possible instances of insult or extortion faced by the more privileged classes. However, when the same world is consumed as a public show by audiences, the enormous, striking incongruity of the depravity of conspicuously privileged classes under liberalization and the deprivation of others may be easily ignored. Middle-class participants may thus see that at least on television, everything is in its place, and everyone is happy, well-fed, and represented.

Thus, even if the public is a "consumer fiction" in some ways, what is important is that it represents to audiences a sense of belonging with a community that, under capitalism and modernity, is perhaps easier to find on television rather than among the "real" public. One participant describes it:

> Actually what happens, while seeing this, watching *Public Demand*, we also involve in that particular clipping, why because, if somebody asks something about day-to-day life, general questions, we also give much preference to watch that. At the same time, also some involvement is there. At the same time, we can get the bliss also, if they are saying some right or wrong by seeing their laughing and saying this and that, we also get some feeling. (Murali)

The feeling of community is perhaps the most useful way to understand how television and the discourse of the public appropriate the need for self-representation, a need that also arises in the context of globalization as a heightened sense of national identity, as I will show in the following chapter. The role of countdowns and public shows in India may thus be seen in the context of liberalization as one of naturalization, as well. However, it is not only the naturalization of certain conventions in watching music television as described in the previous chapter that is relevant here, but the *naturalization of a certain sense of reality itself*. Thus, if privileged classes in India increasingly live their lives in a "landscape," as Kaviraj (1998) claims, countdowns and public shows certainly play an important role in its construction. In other words, these programs capture audiences' sense of need for self-representation and community that arises from the rigors of daily life in a competitive urban environment and present an appropriately sanitized worldview to impose on that environment. The effect of these discourses may be seen as an imposition of meaning, not so much on audiences as passive recipients, but precisely through the authority that audiences assume through these discourses, as an imposition of meaning on their sense of everyday reality itself—a reality that manifests very plainly in Indian everyday life as people and the patterns of privilege that relate them to one another.

CHAPTER 4

GLOBALIZATION AND THE NATION

... in all of the world I'm yet to see another India
—"I love my India" from the Hindi film *Pardes* (foreign)
(translated by author)

One nation. Someday, one world. India. That's who we are.
—Pop singer Shaan in a televised concert

It would not be an overstatement to say that music television, more than any other form of media, has provided Indian audiences with the cultural resources for a popular understanding of what globalization means. While neither music television nor audiencehood are the only conditions for the experience and understanding of globalization in India, there has been a profusion since the early 1990s of music videos and film songs that express, in their lyrics and imagery, ideas and feelings about being Indian in an increasingly interactive and comparative international context.

These songs, and their location in a televisual context marked by a selfconscious hybridity, have clearly not passed unnoticed by participants in this study. While working-class participants once again did not engage with themes of globalization in the interviews, the discussion of Alisha's *Made in India* by middle-class participants showed a depth of reading, interest, and emotional investment that belied what I thought was the somewhat simplistic and sloganistic message in the video. Indian music television audiences, it appears, are indeed seeking to be "global," but on terms that are more complex than an institutional or textual analysis could have predicted. Once again, these terms do not support a celebration of audience resistance, but instead draw attention to how far critical media studies would need to go in understanding the nature of hegemony under globalization.

The preferred meaning of globalization in Indian music television reverses the widespread assumption of globalization as a process of foreign (and particularly Western) incursion. Although the "invasion" metaphor, and the phrase "cultural imperialism" had some public currency in the 1990s (prior to the Indianization phase of satellite television), these ideas have since declined, if not altogether disappeared, in mainstream media discourses. Most of the participants, for instance, despite being educated, well-informed, and critical in some ways, said that they had never heard the phrase "cultural imperialism"—although they all had much to say about the phrase "globalization." With the notable exception of two graduate art students who said quite plainly that globalization was "American colonialism" that was especially harmful to Indian farmers (one of these students belonged to a family of farmers), most middle-class participants characterized globalization as India—Indian people, Indian culture, Indian media, Indian products, Indian services—going out into the world, and the world-stage, as it were.

Such a perception is quite widespread, at the outset, in media institutions. Music television producers and artists often express, either in their marketing strategies (which are also shaped by the growing importance of the Indian diasporic markets in North America, Europe, the Middle East, and Southeast Asia) or in their ideals and hopes, the idea of spreading Indian culture globally. These export-oriented strategies and longings (combined with the tendency of global media and consumer companies to send their American-born Indian employees back to work in their emerging Indian operations) often manifest themselves in the kind of themes that Indian media discourses in general and music television in particular portray. Some of the most popular Hindi films in recent years, for instance, are about Indians living in other countries, or the experience of foreign-returned Indians. Even if films do not explicitly engage with such issues, it has almost become essential for at least one song in most big-budget films to be pictured in foreign locations. In addition, music-based programs like *Antakshari* have also filmed episodes with Indian participants in Dubai and elsewhere. However, it is more than production locations which may be shaping popular perceptions of globalization.

In music videos, film songs, promos, and advertisements, there are a number of ways in which the national and the global are narratively connected. In *Made in India*, which I examine in detail later in this chapter, a fairy-tale setting sets the stage for a princess to turn down suitors from all over the world and choose an Indian man. In the song "I love my India" from the film *Pardes*, a wealthy expatriate patriarch sings the glories of India to his young America-enamored relatives. Outside the purview of music television, advertising celebrates global India in all sorts of ways. One fashion brand announces that it is "Just like America," while another brand says, "Not like America, thankfully." An infomercial in the regional language channel Asianet celebrates the impending wedding of a Kerala boy to a Caucasian woman charmingly bedecked in Indian clothes.

These examples say a great deal about the kind of stories about globalization that Indian media audiences may be encountering in their daily lives. As will be shown in this chapter, the significance of the meanings made by audiences in relation to such discourses derives not so much from audiences' cognitive understanding of the term "globalization" (which may or may not even be relevant), but from the fact that these meanings arise about and within a context of intense transformation in social reality and everyday experience—which, as a whole, may be theorized as "globalization." Given the immensity and complexity of the condition it seeks to describe (and prescribe), the discourse of globalization is caught up perhaps more than any other current discourse in the politics of the "image" (Yoshimoto, 1996).

Due to the centrality of mediation in the experience and understanding of globalization, questions about how globalization is being represented in the media and how its meanings are negotiated by audiences are especially relevant. As Marjorie Ferguson's (1992) important essay on the "Mythology about Globalization" has shown, a number of popular media myths have already become quite widespread in the United States, articulating, under terms like "New World Order," ill-founded ideals about democracy, trade, the disappearance of time and space, and the triumph of communications. The myths about globalization in the Indian media may also derive from the same kind of mandate for "globalization [as] a teleological doctrine that promotes . . . an interlocking system of world trade" (p. 87). However, in the context of reception, it would seem that globalization is experienced and understood in more complex ways than the myths hold, raising the challenge of how globalization could also perhaps be reimagined as something more than an ideological distraction for its undeniably real political economy.

Made in India, Sold on the World

At the time of this study, the celebration of global and national themes on music television had reached a crescendo. To mark India's 50th independence day celebrations on August 15, 1997, a slew of music videos, albums, and retrospective cassette boxed sets of nationalistic film songs were released. The new music videos included a series on Doordarshan sponsored by Coca Cola which were described as a celebration of "the India of the 90s: liberal, assertive, and sexy" (Sethi, 1997, p. 9) in a far cry from the reverential mother goddess iconography for the nation, which used to be the norm in Indian cinema.

The advertising, music, and television businesses also undertook another venture that was quite extraordinary in its scale and imagination, the *Vande Mataram*[1] project. This project centered around an album of the same title composed by A. R. Rahman produced by Sony, and featured a spectacular music video for the song "Maa Tujhe Salaam" ("Mother, Salutations to You"). In addition, a number of corporate-sponsored interviews with national and international celebrities (Nobel Peace Prize winners Nelson Mandela, Yasir Arafat, Shimon Peres, and others) and hundreds of ordinary Indians, were broadcast as well.

Although the main music video from this project did not address global themes as such (instead, it featured giant flags and rows of diverse Indians in deserts), the whole project was situated as both an international and an intergenerational one. Bharat Bala, who directed the project with his wife, explained that he wanted to make the whole word realize the spirit of "Vande Mataram," and to recognize that spirit as "India's property" (Bhatia, 1997). In addition, he wanted that spirit to be conveyed to the young, seeing his role as that of a mediator between his father's freedom-fighting generation and the young Indians of today (Brijnath and Chopra, 1997). Young Indians certainly connected with it, and in addition to the instant success of the album (it beat Elton John's tribute to Diana in the process), it was apparent in the months that followed that "Vande Maataram" had become a catch-all phrase in everyday life.

The implications of *Vande Mataram's* youth-oriented and globally positioned music video nationalism may be better appreciated in the context of the popular reception of a video that had actually inaugurated the whole phenomenon—Alisha's *Made in India*. *Made in India* was the first Indian pop album to be sold on a scale comparable to Hindi film music albums, and the music video for the title song was among the first popular Indian music videos. Although the video was not in active rotation around the time of this study, its pervasiveness was evident. "Made in India" had become a successful concept; it appeared in advertisements, and MTV India used it as the name of one of its programs. In addition, regional variations had also been spawned—a Telugu song called "Made in Andhra" celebrated the ruffled *craaphu* (haircut) and crumpled clothes of the "Made in Andhra student." The most telling sign of its pervasiveness, however, was the fact that

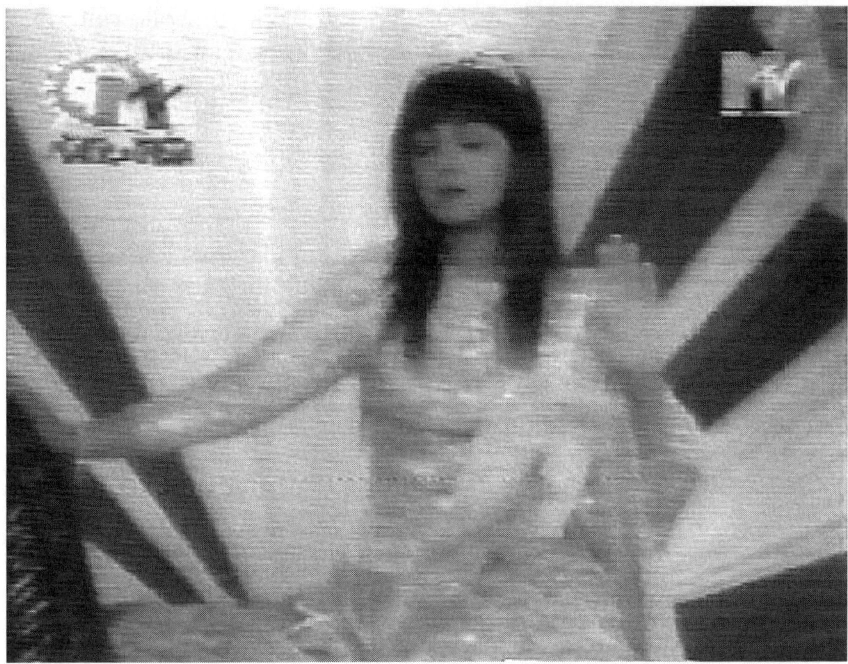

FIGURE 7 Princess Alisha spurns yet another global suitor in "Made in India."

nearly all the participants in this study (except the working-class parents) had seen this video, and most of them said that they liked it very much.

Made in India stages international competition, national pride, and notions of love and marriage to an infectious beat and colorful images, and the import of its meanings may be noted in the fact that it was the first expression in Indian popular culture about the changes Indians had begun to witness in the early 1990s. The lyrics of the song narrate the feelings of a protoganist who says that she has seen the whole world and is now seeking a man with a good heart—which for her means one that is "made in India." The video, directed by Ken Ghosh, provides a colorful narrative, with Alisha playing a fairy-tale princess who is wooed by suitors from different parts of the world. She turns them all down, and in despair turns to a magician who produces an image of her perfect man in a smoky cauldron. Finally, to the accompaniment of both traditional and ambiguously ethnic dancers, snake charmers, twisted yoga practitioners, elephants and tigers, Alisha falls in love with her dream man, who arrives in a box labeled "Made in India."

In general, participants said that they valued the song for its originality, meaningful lyrics, and for the technical sophistication of the video. In terms of the meaning of the song, it is apparent from the following comment that it is seen as being a song about Indian culture in an international context even for a participant who says he may not understand it fully because he does not understand Hindi.

> I thought that from the song, it talks about culture, our Indian culture. Something, saying that Made in India, Made in India. At the same time, they are showing clippings of that Kathakali (classical dance form from Kerala), arts which are famous in India. At the same time they are comparing with Western also, with Japan, Russia, like that. Actually, I can't understand the full meaning of the song. I am very poor in Hindi. But I like this song. Why? Because the music was good, the visual was also very good. (Murali)

This participant constructs the meaning of the song as being about Indian culture in a comparative global context, although he says he does not understand the language of the lyrics very well, suggesting that this meaning is perhaps enabled in no small part by the specific images used in the video, which are recognized by him as being "Indian" and "Western." While I will address the role of these images shortly, what is important at the outset is the fact that participants clearly *feel* represented in this song, as the following comments also suggest:

> They showed our Indian culture very nicely. (Sandhya) (translated from Telugu)

> A proud song. (Kamala)

However, the positive evaluations that these participants have of the song cannot be ascribed to an abstract or sloganistic sense of national pride alone. In response to the question "Do you think this is a patriotic song?" a number of participants said that it was a true representation of being Indian and not "patriotic," which they said referred to what Doordarshan and the government told them to feel. It is clear from the following statements that patriotism is seen as a paternalistic imperative that people ostensibly do not like, as opposed to simply "feeling" Indian, which people clearly do:

> That is, they tell us about worshipping the nation but not about the feeling, the Indian feeling. (Ramesh) (translated from Telugu)

> Not a patriotic song, but has a lot of meaning in it. (Ajay)

> Patriotic song means something like *Jana Gana Mana* (the national anthem). (Nisha)

The popular resonance of *Made in India* may therefore be seen not only in its emotional appeal, but also in the fact that it is seen as representing Indians as they really are, or like to think they are—as opposed to "patriotic" songs, which presumably do not have "a lot of meaning" in them as the above participant would say. In addition, *Made in India* is also implicitly seen as Indians speaking to themselves in a way that they would not find unusual. The injunction to be patriotic is, in contrast, named as an injunction. As one of the above participants says, the problem with such discourses is that "they tell us" about having to revere the nation, but do not simply depict the Indian "feeling" as *Made in India* does. The commercial interests that underlie *Made in India* are, however, not seen as any such "they."

At the heart of these distinctions is the question of the "feeling" that participants describe in the context of the song. While it may be true that "patriotism" suggests discourses that are unable to represent these feelings, these feelings are still connected to a self-perception of national identity. The feeling of national pride that accompanies participants' comments about this song is best appreciated in the light of two interrelated aspects, as the following statement suggests. The first aspect is that these feelings are seen not so much as an audience reaction to national symbols, but instead as the *song's ability to represent these feelings that already exist among Indians.* The second relevant aspect of this process is the fact these feelings are located by participants not in distant symbols of national pride like historical monuments or (more recently) nuclear technology, but instead in the relational and emotional terms of marriage and family:

> When you see the song, the feeling comes. The feeling that it is about this country. The feeling that among all the husbands in the world it is the Indian husband who loves the most. That sort of feeling comes because of watching this song. Even now, that's what I felt. (Raja) (translated from Telugu)

This comment is illustrative because it touches on themes that other participants discuss at length as well, particularly the notions of what being "Indian," being in love, or getting married mean. In addition, this comment also emphasizes the fact that the values that the video embodies in relation to the above themes are not merely understood cognitively, but are experienced with some emotional intensity as well.

Other participants give a name to this emotional intensity-centered subjectivity by using the Hindi word *dil* (heart) or, its Telugu equivalent, *manassu*, as the following statements indicate:

> She is singing the song for the country, about all the important things in our country. Like *kaala ho ya gora* [whether dark or fair] people have *dil*. She is singing about what is important, What are Indians? Our *dil*. (Kiran) (translated from Hindi)

> The richness of Indian tradition, their culture, their customs. And that, what you feel about their *dil*, how, it is. (Lakshmi)

These statements suggest that the reception of the song may indicate not so much of a reaction to the nationalistic overtures of the song as the fact that the song's narrative emphasis on the notion of the heart is recognized by participants as being representative of their own relational and emotional values, and this recognition is in turn articulated in terms of national pride. In other words, being a "husband" (to invoke the comment from above) precedes being "national," and these are both then used to construct a contextual sort of being "global" as well—as illustrated in one of the above participant's statements that "among all the husbands in the world it is the Indian husband who loves the most."

Character and Place

The articulation of relational values with national identities and global awareness suggests a degree of self-relativization rather than an essentialist assertion of Indian supremacy. The lyrics of the song do not simply declare that the Indian heart is the best one in the world, and this part of the narrative is meaningfully engaged with by some participants. The lyrics suggest that Alisha wants a husband with a good heart and it just turns out that an Indian would have a good heart. Thus, as one participant notes, the video does not make the claim that Alisha chooses the Indian simply because he is Indian, but because of his heart:

> She wants someone, [with] all the qualities, whatever, are there, she, like, an Indian has that. She wanted to portray that. She wants a person from anywhere in the world, any corner in the world, but that person should possess the qualities she wants. (Nisha)

In addition, as another participant observes, Alisha's choice comes not necessarily from a blind faith in Indians but from the fact that:

> She doesn't want any, you know, *upar upar ka dikhava* [superficiality]. [She would] like someone natural [and] wants the husband to be very nice. (Ramya)

This comment illustrates the logic of the song, although most participants do not actually problematize it. The narrative of the song does not directly exhort the superiority of Indian culture in an international context, but merely sets it up, in true liberalization style, as one among many competitors in an international marketplace. This imagined global marriage bazaar may be seen by participants as being meritocratically infallible, for it ensures that the best person—in this case, the Indian—wins. The story is also described by one participant as a *swayamvaram* (a practice often mentioned in Indian folklore, in which a princess would choose her suitor), drawing parallels between the worlds of tradition and contemporary globalization. In this context, Alisha's ability to choose her partner in *Made in India* has also been seen by some scholars as an example of the assertion of "feminine desire" in a media context where women are often portrayed as objects of male desire (Curtin, 1999).

Although participants, male and female, did not mention Alisha's royally autonomous position in the narrative as an example of female agency, some participants did engage with the question of whether she was being true to her own premises. In the following exchange among a group of female high school students, participants confront an apparent contradiction between what the lyrics of the song were saying and how Alisha actually goes about making her choice, and end up affirming the universal ideals that underpin the whole practice of finding the right person:

> Mamatha: She's saying "Made in India" but choosing a guy who doesn't look Indian.
>
> Nisha: But those qualities can be in many other people who are not Indians. They can be much better than an Indian person.
>
> Maya: There are many people outside who have a much better heart than Indians.
>
> Kartika: It's not compulsory that an Indian's heart is only good. You know, a foreigner can be much better than an Indian. *It doesn't matter which place you are [from] it's the character that's important.* (emphasis added)

This exchange shows that at least some participants find the ideals embodied in Alisha's character to be universal, not necessarily identical to being Indian. On this note, one of these participants also observes that

Alisha is actually not being true to her premise by choosing the Indian man without getting to know him:

> He just comes out of a box, she doesn't even know what his nature is and all that stuff, she just sort of likes him and that's it. Now they are married. (Nisha)

Alisha's selection of the Indian suitor (played by model Milind Soman) is laden with ironies that point not only to the narrative inconsistencies as these are perceived by participants, but also to the limits and assumptions implicit in the mandate and mechanisms of emerging forms of representing nationality in popular media discourses. Alisha is faulted in the comment above for choosing someone without getting to know him—by implication—choosing someone only because of his looks or origin. In a sense, this is seen as contradicting the noble universal sentiments underlying her romantic quest. These sentiments, as some of the above statements indicate, would have to do with liking someone who is "natural" and has a good character. According to the above discussion, it also implies that valuing such sentiments would mean not being parochial and accepting the idea that good values could be present in anyone, and not only an Indian.

This discussion therefore indicates some degree of self-relativization among these participants. They are clearly open to the idea that Indians may not be the only people who can claim to have a good character. However, even as the premise of the video as one that privileges character over superficial "looks" is thus accepted, the issue of appearance does remain pertinent, given the fact that the video constructs much of the narrative through its visual codes (for instance, viewers are fairly straightforwardly told that the man she chooses is Indian because he is carried into the palace in a box marked "Made in India").

Looking Indian

Even as the narrative structure of the song, with its emphasis on character, is reproduced in terms of what may be described as the egalitarian and meritocratic ideologies of liberalization and globalization, the role of specific images in this process remains important. While the profusion of images in the video enforce what may be characterized as the normalization of looking in music television, what is relevant here is not only the nuances of knowing national and global identities through visual recogni-

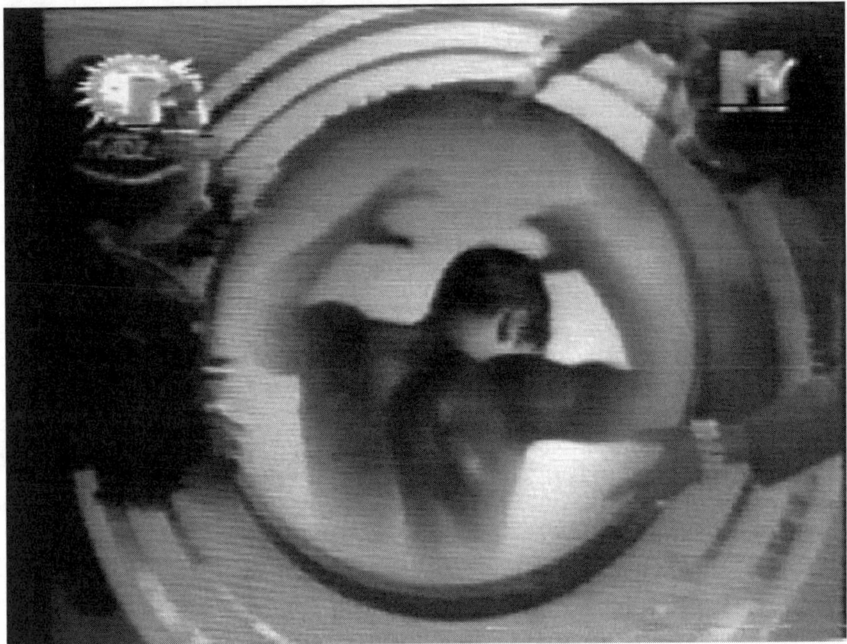

FIGURE 8 Alisha sees the man she will choose for a husband in a magician's cauldron. He is then brought to her palace in a box labeled "Made in India."

tion, but the variations among participants in terms of access to visual competences as well. For instance, how would participants know that a certain suitor was, say, "American"? What presumptions would they make about Alisha's own nationality in the video? How would their knowledge of certain visual codes affect their investment in the representations in the video?

In response to questions about what seemed "Indian" about the video, a number of participants indicate that the man Alisha chooses does not actually "look Indian." On the one hand, most participants know that he is Indian, not only from within the narrative, but also because they recognize the actor. However, his looks are problematized:

> He looks more like, you know, probably an American [-born] Indian. He doesn't look much like an Indian. (Mamatha)

In addition, Alisha's appearance also confounds an easy ascription of nationality. Her multiple costumes and wigs are interpreted in various ways:

Her dressing, short blond hair [suggest she is Western]. (Mamatha)

When we watch this clipping, we can see that the way of dressing is Western style like that royal coat, then that gown. That one is a gown, we can easily say that it is not the Indian culture, it is Western-based culture. (Murali)

Being a blonde [was very Western]. (Bhanu)

While the above participants merely identify images that looked non-Indian, the following participant finds these images quite offensive, given the context of the meaning of the song:

I don't like the video. It's very bad to talk about "Made in India" and . . . go on wearing foreign clothes and put on blonde hair and all that. Crazy. (Padma)

At the same time, another participant attempts to situate Alisha's non-Indian appearance in the video in terms of the song's narrative:

Maybe she is trying to show she's from some other country but she wants Indian, something like that, looks like that. The way she was dressed up, she looked like an Arabic [*sic*]. (Arun)

However, not all participants see Alisha as portraying a non-Indian character, as the following examples show:

[She looks] Indian. (Jaya)

Modern Indian. (Praveen)

Indian imitating the Western style. (Mohan)

While Alisha is thus perceived for the most part as an Indian who is either portraying other nationalities or is merely being cosmopolitan, one set of implications of such readings is evident in the following statement. Like some of the participants who had made inferences in the context of countdowns about other viewers on the basis of their readings of the texts (Chapter 3), the following participants also derive some ideas about Alisha's audience on the basis of her appearance:

She was catering to the global audience. That's why she was not looking Indian. (Naresh)

A similar notion is conveyed in the following statement as well. For this participant, Alisha's perceivedly Western appearance is a concession made by her for pleasing her audience, which may or may not be global, but needs a Western image all the same:

> The thought behind her is very good. She wanted to tell about the Indianness, Indian people, Indian tradition and the Indian customs and all those. But as well as, she's also concentrated on the public taste and she presented in the Western style. (Kamala)

These statements illustrate the relevance not only of what participants value in the meaning of the video in its representations of nationality or character, but also of the specific role of visualization in constructing such meanings. While the overall response to the music video for many participants is an emotional one that enacts a feeling of national identity and community, the discussions about how characters in the video looked draw attention to the complexities involved in reception as a visual experience. The responses to questions about the visual aspects of the video are thus best understood in relation not only to the specific images that are used in the video, but also to the specific burden of representation that they carry.

In other words, the fact that certain images are perceived by participants as representing something called the "global," "national," or "traditional" draws attention not only to the fact that these images merely represent these things, but also to the possibility that these images may serve to concretize the experiences that participants may characterize as "global," "national," or "traditional" into a visualized sense of naturalness.

There are some indications that visualization is understood as being somehow more facile in global representations than in national ones. For instance, the above comment suggests that Alisha's looks were constructed in a particular manner that was more suitable to the global audience. Underlying this observation is not only the sense that not having an Indian look makes Alisha global, but also the assumption that there is a global audience for her music video. Such an assumption recurs frequently in participants' discussion of this video. It may indicate the emergence of a notion of the global audience among participants that is based on an assumption of who else may be watching—simply because what people in India are watching *looks like* it could be watched elsewhere as well. For instance, there is a perception among some participants that the audio of *Made in India* is national but the video is international.

At the same time, participants have no doubt that some of the images in the video are fundamentally Indian, even characterizing them as one participant does as "striking images of totally traditional India" (Padma).

Specifically, participants mention the following details as "being Indian" in the video:

> The Kathakali dancers . . . and the dancers behind also. They dressed them, kind of traditionally. (Jyothi)

> The palace set, dance movements, the whole set appears Indian. (Raja) (translated from Telugu)

> That Bharatanatyam (classical dance from Tamil Nadu). (Ajay)

The dancers and the dances, in addition to the sets, strike these participants not only as Indian, but also implicitly as traditional, to the extent that both Bharatanatyam and Kathakali are classical South Indian dance forms. The fact that certain images are recognized not only as Indian but also as representations of certain Indian traditions, indicates both the participant's access to such competences that are needed to make such a recognition, and also the fact that these images do indeed represent something meaningful.

The Burden of Recognition

At the outset, there are different ways in which the dances could be decoded as "Indian"—in terms of costumes, makeup, movements, and so on. For a person with a greater knowledge of and investment in these dance forms, such as the following participant who is a dance student, the same representations could also be problematic:

> Because when they're showing about the Indian dances and all, they're showing Kathakali and all. But regarding the Kuchipudi (classical dance from Andhra Pradesh) they are not clear-the dress is not *pucca* (perfect), traditional way in which the other girls are wearing. *Because when the layman abroad, they see, they think that this is a particular dress you're wearing in India but that's not true.* The Indian classical dancers won't wear that kind. Those kinds of dresses. Sleeveless and all. So maybe sometimes it's misleading people. And trying to portray the classical dances, Shiva's dance, that is okay, Kathakali costume is shown, that is okay. But regarding the other girls, group of girls, wearing the costumes, it is not good. (Anjali) (emphasis added)

While this criticism is not widespread among participants, it is important because it shows the sense of investment that some audience members would have in the representational premise of certain images. The participant quoted above is especially concerned that those who would not know better, for instance, viewers of this video abroad, would end up mistaking what is an arbitrary construction in the video for an authentic Indian cultural form. Once again, there is an assumption here that the video would be watched by audiences outside India, and her sense of who she is is clearly troubled by the inappropriateness of the dancers in the video ("sleeveless" may also suggest the dancers' clothes are seen as being too revealing).

These concerns raise the question of what indeed the video does represent. With the exception of the unmistakably unique costume and mask of the Kathakali dancer, the other dancers' costumes do not necessarily mark them as belonging to any specific dance tradition. It may be noted that no other participant in fact perceives the group dancers in particular as Kuchipudi dancers. Their costumes, in fact, do not seem to adhere to any particular dance form and suggest a loosely constructed fashion (orange and saffron turbans, for instance) that may be characterized as an emerging Indian music video ethnic-chic. However, this participant perceives them as Kuchipudi dancers, perhaps from certain dance gestures that she may know better, and then expresses her concern at their lack of authenticity.

Her concern exemplifies two important and related points. The video is perceived by her as not only representing Indian culture, but as representing Indian culture *in the manner that she also thinks it is being represented to a global audience*. The second relevant point is that her concern highlights how at least some audience members would be distressed by the fact that false or inaccurate representations could be taken to be true by those who did not know better. In other words, she does not like the possibility that a false representation (of her or her culture) could become widespread globally.

Such a possibility is not far-fetched, given the kind of images that are used to represent India in the video. The orientalistic manner in which elephants, tigers, and snakecharmers are used in this video may serve to press an alien image of India into the imagination of Indian audiences—although the orientalists in this case are not European colonizers. However, most participants do not seem to think that there is anything alien about choosing such images to represent India. On one occasion, a participant said that the video looked like "an American's view of India," but was challenged by her friends, who thought it was quite an authentic self-representation.

The fact that most participants think that the video indeed does represent an Indian view of India attests to the degree to which what at least one participant sees as an alien view is naturalized. Again, this participant does not say that the video is not Indian, or that these images do not represent India. Her position is merely that these images show how India is traditionally represented in and by and for the West. However, most participants do not make such a distinction within the representation, and accept it as an evocative self-representation. While the presence of snakecharmers and elephants in India may thus enable participants to gloss over the selective nature of such images, it is also instructive to note that even some outright fantasy images suggest India to the following participant:

> And that mythical man . . . he showed that image of an Indian male in that pot with steam coming up, that is typically oriental. You can limit that particular scene to Indian origin. (Vijay)

Thus, even a mere swirl of smoke rising from a soothsayer's cauldron invokes a uniquely "oriental" or "Indian" experience for this participant. This aspect of the video may be recognized as Indian by him because of certain competences that he may have had prior access to, but what is also worth exploring is the possibility that such a representation in this video may serve to channelize his broader experience of being Indian not only into that particular representation, but also into a naturalization of the reception of that representation as a heightened experience of being Indian. In the process, the imagery and discourses of orientalism that constitute the specific kind of cultural competence in evidence here are further strengthened and naturalized.

In short, the reception of *Made in India* suggests that participants in general recognize themselves through the representations of the nation and tradition in the video, even if some of these representations are arguably orientalistic and self-exoticizing. In other words, audiences do not feel that an alien image of themselves is being imposed upon them. On the contrary, their ability to recognize themselves in such representations seems to fit in with a larger emerging perception that they are indeed being watched by the rest of the world as well.

Desperately Seeking NRIs

While these participants assume that the video is made, rather successfully at that, for a global audience on the basis of its specific representations of

India, other participants assume a global role for the video, specifically in the context of its reception among non-resident Indians (NRIs). The centering of a global awareness around the presence of Indian nationals living abroad by participants is not confined to *Made in India*, and suggests once again the ways in which nationality is situated on favorable terms in relation to globalization in everyday discourses. To some extent, the presence of NRIs does play a role in affecting what Indian audiences see, given the fact the overseas market for Indian cultural products is quite a valuable one as well (Pendakur & Subramanyam, 1996). On this note, the following participant's observation that *Made in India* was made primarily for an NRI audience is not unfounded:

> Basically this song when it was thought of and made, it was aimed towards NRIs that too those, as far as my recollection is, I don't think I'm correct cent percent but they wanted to show this video, this video was specifically made for NRIs and in U.S. it made good sales and review *manchiga ochindi* [was good]. *Manchitanam endante* [The nice thing about this video is that], it reminds me of Indian soil. Made in India. Something made in India. And just imagine, a counterpart made in India. People are going and settling outside India and they are searching for a counterpart made in India. (Vijay)

A similar point is made by another participant, who sees *Made in India*'s message as being quite relevant to NRIs, who may get to see people from all over the world, but finally want to get married to someone from India:

> What she wants to highlight is, even after seeing people from other lands, she thinks India is the best one and wherever it may be, an Indian is the best person when it really comes down to settling in life also. Many NRIs now want Indians to be their partners also. (Naresh)

While the above participants situate *Made in India*'s global significance in terms of the marital aspirations of NRIs, which are a frequent subject of media attention in India as well (D'Souza, 1992), another participant assumes a more general NRI audience for "Made in India" on the basis of the fact that certain TV game shows are frequently filmed in foreign locations with participation by NRIs:

> In the [United] States also, so many Indians are there. So they may also like it. Because, see, I saw on *Antakshari*, so, so many Indians, when Renuka and Annu Kapoor [TV hosts] went there. So these songs are very proud for them because it's Indian songs and they prefer so much for that. (Pragathi)

The presence of Indians living abroad is noted by the participants here with different forms of national identification. The main implication of these observations, in the light of the prevalent themes about NRIs in Indian media discourses, seems to be that they have been successful in the West and have also maintained their cultural traditions—and culture and prosperity have somehow produced each. Once again, the theme of globalization as a simultaneous strengthening of the nation's role—economically and culturally—in the world is evident here, although in this case the "mediascape" is given its value in the terms of the "ethnoscape," to use Appadurai's (1990) terms. To summarize, the assumption here seems to be that since Indians are going all over the world, so must Indian television programs.

Location and Global Audiencehood

In addition to the assumptions about global audiences that underlie some of the responses to *Made in India*, the notion of a global audience was also discussed at length by participants in response to a question about whether they felt in general that they were a part of a global audience. Once again, the more widespread assumption here seems to be not so much that they are a part of a global audience because they are watching Western programming, but that what they are watching in India—mostly Indian programs—are being watched around the world as well. As one participant notes:

> Like STAR TV is okay [not surprising as an example of a channel with a global audience], but for example Zee TV. Basically it was Indian but now we get the feeling that they are showing our programs to Europe, U.S., everywhere it's being shown. It has increased. That is the best way. We are part of the international audience. (Arun)

While it is true that Zee TV is available via satellite in Europe and North America, the assumption seems to be that all audiences abroad have mainstream access to Indian programming in the same manner that audiences in India do. This is certainly not the case, given the fact that overseas broadcasts of Indian programs are marginal in relation to domestic programming. However, for this participant, such an assumption forms a broader understanding of the term "globalization" itself, which he defines as:

> Not restricting to one place. It's like opening up to the widest possible range, that is the globalization. When talking about the Indian serials, the

way we make our serials, there's quite a lot of difference between those people and what we make. So people have started appreciating our own serials. They like it. The emotions in the serial. So it has globalized, the Indian culture has been globalized. People like it. And they have, many people have adapted it. It's good. For instance, Indians who have left our country are staying there again they want to see the Indian program, we get to see it. (Arun)

While the sense of a global community in these examples is closely related to the outward expansion of the national community through migration and through media, the following participant enthusiastically embraces the concept of a global audience without any qualifications in terms of nationality:

> In general, in every walk of life I feel like I'm a global audience. In every way. In the newspapers also you can see most of the news outside India so I feel even if I read the news, as if I'm a global audience. What you find happening in the world. (Samir)

It is not just his ability to relate to events in other countries that enable this viewer to make this claim, but also his explicit imagining that there are other people such as himself elsewhere relating to the same things on the media:

> I feel part of a world, all over the globe. I represent a particular part of India but I feel as if I'm audience all over the world. Because there might be some people also all over the world, globe, who think the same way. (Samir)

Another participant supports the notion of belonging to a global audience as well, although he qualifies his definition of a global audience on the basis of the channels:

> The concept of global audience depends on [the] channel you are seeing. Not all the channels are global channels, not music channels. Definitely when you are seeing that channel, the Telugu channel, you're part of your own state. Not even the other states maybe. Of course, this BBC, CNN, you're seeing, you're regularly seeing that. That is global audience. (Vijay)

While this participant says that it is possible to clearly distinguish global, national, and regional levels of location as an audience member on the basis of the channels he is watching, another participant, whose family primarily watches regional channels, says that she finds it interesting that she feels part of a global audience even when watching regional channels:

> If we watch Zee TV and all [it's understandable that] we feel like that [global] but we watch all the Telugu channels and all we feel like we are interacting with all international things. We feel it's global. And in my house we always watch Telugu channels. (Anjali)

This observation highlights the fact that the identification of global, regional, and the national levels to the audience are not restricted to the geographic reach of the channel or its language. As the above participant claims, it is possible even for a predominantly regional channel viewer to feel global as well—a possibility supported by the prevalence not only of advertisements for global brands and foreign programs dubbed into Telugu, but also in the frequent invocation of global themes in the lyrics and imagery of film songs. For instance, a Telugu film song on the charts at the time of this study featured the refrain "I am Lotus, You are Microsoft," underscoring the resonances that the global information technology industry has found in the local context of Andhra Pradesh.[2]

While the regional and the global are thus articulated for one participant, the rise of satellite channels is seen by the following participant as enabling primarily an increase in national cohesion through an increased awareness of regional diversity, with a global sensibility being an occasion-specific phenomenon:

> Because of the satellite channels I think we are having more exposure to all parts of the country, all the cultures, before that it wasn't like that. It was very restricted. For instance, you can concentrate more on the national aspect. International, okay, depends on that date. (Bhanu)

While all of the above statements suggest a fair degree of certainty by participants about their location as global, national, and regional audiences, the following statement expresses various doubts that the participant has about nationality and globality in the experience of television. He initially situates himself as a member of a global audience which, as he qualifies, does not mean that he becomes transnational. Instead, he becomes more conscious about his own and others' nationalities. At the same time, as he says, he thinks that this consciousness is a purely intellectual one, or at least, he tries to make sure that it is, lest he "lose his nationality":

> I feel like part of international audience but at the same time I feel, I try to see the nationality, I don't want to lose my nationality and find out, what is it that makes him an American or an Englishman, and what is it that which makes me an Indian. Trying to, you know, sort out and think something [but] it's only in the thinking process. (Vijay)

However, he finds a simple solution to such doubts, and then he has little confusion about who he is or where he is:

> As soon as I switch off the TV it goes off. And I forget about everything and become Indian . . . so how you become part of the international audience? You are sitting in India and watching on Indian TV. Indian air. So you don't forget about your basic nationality, whether the program is aired from America or Singapore. (Vijay)

The equation of globalization with television by this participant allows a simple escape from it; when he has had enough, he turns it off and returns to the reality of his location in India. The larger question this raises is fairly simple: can globalization simply be turned off by viewers? While no participant says so, it does seem apparent that the assumption of global identities by viewers in ways that do not disturb a sense of national identity suggests that the impact of television as an agent of globalization is certainly not seen as a cause for alarm. For instance, although participants mention fashions, lifestyles, viewing habits, study habits, and general knowledge as specific areas of life upon which they think the rise of satellite television has had an impact, they do not seem to perceive this or globalization in general as an experience of rapid transformation.

Globalization is for the most part given positive meanings by participants. In some ways, there is no denying the fact that globalization has enabled for audiences a greater sense of representation for the nation in the global context. Most satellite channels aimed at national audiences in India are also widely watched in the Middle East, both by expatriate Indians and by other residents who have long been familiar with Indian cinema. Zee TV broadcasts in Europe and North America, and Sun TV has announced plans to bring a range of South Indian language channels to North America (Govardhan, 1999). The International Channel in the United States features a selection of Channel V's Asian countdowns, including the Indian Top Ten, and Channel V has plans to broadcast in North America, too (Singh, 1999).

Thus, in some ways, Indian television has indeed been globalized. But at the same time, it would seem that the assumptions that underlie participants' understanding of the same process are somewhat exaggerated, not only because of the fact that Indian television programs are clearly not watched by mainstream Western audiences, but also because the terms on which India and the West encounter each other in representation are unequal. For instance, Western pop music videos by Kula Shaker, Meredith Brooks, Michael Jackson, No Doubt, and others that have featured Indian imagery may be seen by Indian audiences as signs of India's recognition in the West (Juluri, 1998b). However, these representations are less the "discovery" of India by Western audiences in the way that Indian audiences believe than an example of brazen and sometimes irreverent exoticization.[3]

The assumption of authority as national subjects by audience members in a global context is thus an assumption, in both senses of the word. On the one hand, it is an assumption because the representations of India that Indian audiences see in their own videos as well as Western videos may either not be widely circulated in the West or simply not recognized in the manner that Indian audiences would like to think they are being recognized. It is also an assumption of authority to the extent that becoming a global audience does entail certain representational opportunities for them as national subjects in a newly emerging global context. In other words, they may indeed feel proud to speak not just as Indians, but as global Indians.

The problem with this situation is the fact that the West remains, even by default, the main source of legitimacy and recognition. Melissa Butcher (1997, p. 17), writing about the Miss World pageant held in Bangalore, critiques the emergence of what she calls the "necessity of our recognition [by non-Indian viewers] as if our existence depended on it."[4] What is curious and troubling about this self-orientalization, though, is the fact that this imagined performance for a global audience is really being put on for the national audience. To summarize, it seems like the present trend for Indian media producers in representing India is to construct images that appear like they are being watched by the rest of the word—even if it is only Indian audiences that are watching them.

Thus, becoming a global audience in India is marked by an apparent contradiction that parallels both uses of the notion of assumption here. On the one hand, it is a legitimate claim for audiences to make that they can be global without necessarily consuming Western media. On the other hand, it is indicative of a renewed capitulation to the West because it is in the presumed recognition by the West that national identity is being affirmed. In other words, it may be fair to say that the self-recognition of audiences in nationalist representations in a global context is not a recognition of the national self in these representations alone, but one in which the *national self is recognized as being recognized by the West*.

Do these assumptions of authority by audience members, as the public in the national context, and as Indians in the international context, constitute evidence of the impact of television in some form? If so, does this impact warrant its characterization as "cultural imperialism"—not necessarily in the terms of its original formulation—but certainly in terms of significance? If cultural imperialism is conceived as a simple replacement of national culture by Western culture, ignoring momentarily the complexities of both terms, then the audience readings discussed in this chapter would not support its existence. At the outset, discourses of globalization in India, as seen in this chapter, clearly do not dwell on the West at the expense of the nation. Moreover, the specific representations of the West in Indian media discourses suggest a more contradictory approach rather than one of complete subservience to it.

However, the problem of cultural imperialism comes not from these instances in themselves, but in the fact that they constitute a broader discourse about globalization in India that is clearly unrepresentative of the political and economic realities of India's relationship with the West. In a surprisingly unashamed instance of this, a print advertisement for a five-star hotel says: "The man from IMF [International Monetary Fund] looked around and said, 'things have changed in your country since my last visit.'—I reckoned the smile was worth a million bucks." What is alarming, however, is not only the fact that this advertisement celebrates the nation's capitulation to the IMF, but the fact that this scenario may well be true; the presence of an excessively luxurious and exorbitantly priced five star hotel in the context of striking poverty all around may actually inspire another "million bucks" from the IMF man, presumably to build more such hotels.

This does not imply, however, that the discourses of globalization in India *only* serve the function of ideological distraction from economic realities. There is no denying the fact that the strength of Indian cultural production has ensured that globalization is not equated with a sweeping sense of Westernization, and that Indian audiences are able to construct their own non-Western global perspectives. The problem is that Indian cultural production, under the aegis of global media organizations, has also been confronted by the poverty of its own imagination in providing self-representation to Indian audiences, not to mention the broader poverty that circles the much sought after middle-class markets in the first place.

The magnitude of this problem can be appreciated not from simply comparing representation and reality, as if the latter were somehow simplistically and totally apprehensible, but from studying how representations of a particular kind become naturalized in their reception by audiences. What audiences say, as in the case of this study, indicates that whatever meanings and values that audiences may claim come about in the light of specific media representations. Neither the celebration of the activity of global audiences, nor the mere inference of cultural effects from the political economy of global media may be helpful, but the meanings made by audiences around certain representations and discourses draw attention to the constructed and arbitrary nature of these representations and discourses as well.

In other words, while media impact may not take the form of a simple line of effect from text to audience, if the meanings made by global audiences can support the charges of cultural imperialism, as I will attempt to show in the next chapter, then the specific representations, and the media that promote them, are important as well. In other words, cultural imperialism need not be cast as so coterminous with capitalism and modernity that reception study is irrelevant to it, as Tomlinson (1991) argues, but must be identified clearly and specifically in reception, and responsibility placed upon the media for its role in constructing such representations.

The problem with these representations is not so much that they cause certain emotional or ideological responses among audience members as the fact that they serve to channelize the meaningful experiences of audience members into these representations. To illustrate, audience members may recognize the feeling that they get when watching *Made in India* as being about themselves, not in the least because it embodies relational values which are also important values in people's everyday lives. They name this feeling as being "Indian," and then go on to say that being Indian is the best thing in the world, at least in terms of the values underlying this feeling. In other words, relational value and emotional experience are channeled by television into certain emerging discourses about globalization and nationality. Similarly, relational value also sustains emerging conceptions of global audiencehood; for instance, the primacy accorded to NRIs in constructing such discourses. At the same time, there is also an assumption that not just NRIs, but the whole world is watching and recognizing, India.

These developments assume greater significance given the specific representations that seem to enable audience members to make such meanings. While it is not the snakecharmer or ethnic dancer alone that may be responsible for the shape of audience readings, it is profoundly troubling that Indian audiences' need for self-representation and recognition is being provided for by television through images such as these. Thus, even as the emerging Indian global consciousness seems to combine a positive spirit of national belonging and universal aspiration, there is no doubt that the use of orientalistic representations such as those in *Made in India* has consequences. The naturalization of these representations through recognition by audience members has two socially and culturally deleterious aspects to it. It not only reinforces certain images which are straight out of the colonizer's imagination as authentic representations, but also restricts other images from acquiring the same representational value. These representations may thus constitute an emerging hegemonic globality among Indian audiences, the consequences of which I will explore in Chapter 5.

CHAPTER FIVE

BECOMING A GLOBAL AUDIENCE

Young people should never challenge their parents' authority;
If people have to succeed in life, they have to be materialistic;
I would consider migrating to the West if the opportunity arose.
—Survey statements with which most young respondents agree[1]

Yesteryear Telugu film songs are like fragrant jasmines floating on the undulating pool of serenity called mind, white as the moonlight.
—A music critic (Madhav, 2002, April 3)

These statements perhaps best capture the conditions of becoming a global audience in relation to music television in India. The core experience of music, film, and television is still perhaps "the pool of serenity" noted above in the case of old film songs, but it is one that is deeply disturbed by the contemporary and contradictory forces that Indians find themselves in as far as careers and families are concerned. If there is one abiding theme in the preceding chapters that is worth recognizing, it is the expression, in a variety of contexts and manners, of a sense of sentimentality anchored in the ties of families, friendships, and relations in general. Watching music television has involved the naturalization of various practices specific to the postglobalization forms of music television, but the content of music television has not strayed far from the world of singing brothers, sisters, parents, children, husbands/wives, and more recently boyfriends/girlfriends of Indian cinema and television. Watching music countdown programs has entailed audience investment in an egalitarian sense of the "public" that normalizes domestic exoticization and the evacuation of accountability from social relations; but watching the public is also about the "craziness" or "bliss" (to use participants' words) of being among, with, and most importantly *for* people in everyday life. Watching videos like *Made in India*, which celebrate being Indian in direct relation to the rest of the world, has been at the center of a misplaced sense of global recognition that is alarming in its chosen ignorance about India's place in the world; but also affirming in its innocence about the values of being "a good husband" (participant's phrase), no matter where one is from.

This chapter is an attempt to recognize this sentimentality for what it says about globalization by situating it not so much as a pristine, nationally bounded condition encroached upon by global modernity, but instead as a meaningful understanding of universal social conditions that has emerged in the present context in the throes of a particular encounter with modern globality. In other words, the great Indian sentiment is best treated not as some national-cultural trait (although media discourses may glorify it in those terms), but as one nationally labelled expression of aspirations that are as lofty and humanistic as they are universal. The principal difference here is not one of "Indian" and say, "Western" cultures, but that between modern globality, or the world as it is structured and made sense of by modernity, and another nonmodern globality that is denied its own globality by modernity. This chapter is an attempt to restore such a claim to an alternative globality, and does so by situating audience theories in relation to epistemic critiques of postcoloniality.

What does it mean to become a global audience? At the outset, it is useful to acknowledge that the process of rendering the words of a small number of research participants into a concept called the "audience" is a situated academic practice involving issues of representation, constituency, and struggles over the definition of knowledge. The specific tradition within which this study attempts to do this is what Virginia Nightingale (1996) calls "cultural studies audience research," which has been concerned with issues of popularity, politics, and meaning, and has been based on some form of empirical research. Despite the profound contribution of this line of work to media studies, Nightingale points out that it has also been a victim of the "ideology of the audience enacted in the public and commercial discourses" (p. 147) that has tended to objectify people as audiences. Cultural studies audience research, according to Nightingale, should strive for a more "ecological orientation in which the audience is . . . recognized as an interacting and integral part of the culture" (p. 146).

The audience, in other words, is not a natural phenomenon. A better understanding of the audience may come not from reducing it to a group of people, but from approaching it as a social and historical formation. From a cultural studies perspective, as Nightingale shows, it is useful to recognize the centrality of the text-audience relation in this process, and configure this central relation to a continued empirical project of ethnography and reception studies. Given these qualifications, what would cultural studies have to say about something called the global audience? The marketing-oriented definition of the global audience as a billion people all over the world watching the Olympics or *Baywatch* is clearly not the answer. The question is better served perhaps by asking what the "global" does to the audience-text relation—and by doing so also appreciate what the audience-text relation does to the "global."

The reception of music television in India is therefore not so much about a "global" text and a "local" audience as a transmission-oriented communications perspective may see it, but instead about the construction of a new sense of the "global" under renewed conditions of modernization. The "global," in this sense, does not necessarily have to be seen as meanings about things (such as American music videos) that are "worldwide" in a geographical sense, but as meanings about things (such as emotions and relationships) that can be seen as "universal" (Waters, 1995). In this chapter, I explore the possibilities for the relationally grounded sentimentality expressed by participants in this study to be understood as an alternative universalism to that of social modernity and hence as an alternative, nonmodern globality. Following Roland Robertson (1990), "globality" may be understood not only as a "condition" but as a form of "consciousness" as well. The meanings made in relation to music television in this study may hence be seen not only as meanings of music television, but as meanings of the "world" as well. These meanings are not confined to what educated, middle-class participants say about "globalization" in particular, but encompass a broader and deeper sensibility that is not always expressed in modern discursive terms; and it is the constraints and conditions on the expression of this sensibility that draw attention to the profoundly political nature of globalization as well.

The globalistic aspiration of this sensibility may also be appreciated in Anthony King's observation (1997, p. 10) that "if there are globally produced cultures, there are . . . culturally produced views of globality" as well. From this perspective, becoming a global audience may be seen not only as the outcome of cultural production on a worldwide scale by giant media conglomerates, but as a moment of situated struggle over what constitutes the world for the audience. The "culturally produced views of globality" in this study, as I argue in this chapter, are an articulation of modern globality with a sensibility that is easily seen as nonmodern, but requires a severe political and intellectual investment for its recognition—and reimagination (Appadurai, 1990) as a globality. Central to such a project is a closer examination of the politics of knowledge under globalization, particularly in terms of how "knowledge" emerges at the intersection of the reception practices of audiences and the intellectual practices of audience researchers. As Buell (1994) notes, globalization may hence be seen, in terms of the "rapid alteration in the circulation of knowledge" (p. 337) that emerges in this study in the everyday world of audiences and in the institutional context of global and media studies. I examine each of these aspects in this chapter, beginning with a discussion of the role of knowledge in the reception of music television and concluding with an outline of an alternative understanding of globality that would emerge from the institutional recognition of such knowledge.

The basis for such a move comes from the similarities and differences in the range of cultural competences that may be identified in the readings made by participants in this study. A key difference that is apparent is the absence among working-class participants and some older middle-class participants of the recognition of many of the genre conventions and discourses that other middle-class participants are familiar with. At the same time, working-class and middle-class participants both emphasize the emotional and relational aspects of reception when watching music television. I argue that these patterns derive from differences in the kind of authority that different groups of participants assume in speaking about their reception experiences and that the locations of such authority need to be understood in the epistemic struggles of what postcolonialist writers have called "alternative modernities" (Gaonkar, 1999). These epistemic struggles, in turn, represent not so much of an opposition between the global and the local, as a struggle between different forms of globality within the audience as one important "location" (Hay, 1996) under globalization.

The Social Distribution of Knowledge

An important theoretical concern in this study is the question of apportioning value to what participants say, and are perhaps unable to say, about music television. It is apparent that some participants did not simply know the meanings of various discourses on music television, but watched it and enjoyed it nonetheless. For such participants, perhaps a sense of due importance could be given by acknowledging the representational value of whatever little they did say. To illustrate, one participant spoke very little during the interviews, and seemed rather unconcerned about many of my questions about music television practices. Virtually the only statement he ever made was that the famous maudlin melodrama song "Jagame Maya" (the world is an illusion) from the Telugu film *Devadasu* (1953) was "great." One way of validating this participant's reception experience would be to recognize that not speaking much about music television does not necessarily negate the depth of its experience. Instead, the one statement with which this participant defined himself perhaps represents as much about his reception experience as that of the many engaging statements made by other participants, and acknowledging this in audience analysis would be one useful way of attributing appropriate "weight" to what constitutes knowledge in reception.

Knowledge, in general, is socially segmented among participants. While most participants understood, for instance, the premise of countdown shows and the discourses of globalization implicit in *Made in India*, there were some who did not. The main axis along which such a difference appeared was class, and perhaps, to a lesser extent, generation. Older middle-class participants, for instance, did not seem to identify with some of the themes that younger middle-class participants did, but understood these themes. With working-class participants, however, many of these themes seemed outside their scope of interest and intelligibility and also pointed out, I believe, some of the limitations of my research approach.[2] Without reducing participant readings to their class position, it would be useful however to acknowledge that these readings derive from different kinds of access to the cultural competences involved in the reception of music television. In the present discussion, I would rather characterize the difference in readings and access to cultural competence between those who are "in the know" regarding music television and those who are not, rather than as an essentialist class difference—although this difference is indeed crucially embedded, as Bourdieu (1984) shows, in the broader social distribution of privilege. The ability of certain audience members to understand the meanings of music television genres, for instance, implies that they have access to certain competences that others do not. What does this unequal access say, in the case of this study, about the relationship between knowledge and privilege?

Following Bourdieu, Ellen Seiter (1999) points out that audience studies have often examined the working of "cultural capital" (tastes and knowledge), and how it sometimes translates into "social capital" (status and relationships), but not how these become "symbolic capital" (through their institutional recognition) given the scarcity of institutional settings in which cultural capital about television would be legitimated (p. 26). For the participants in this study who are "in the know," their ability to engage with the discourses not only of music television but globalization (and the interview situation) also constitute cultural capital, and perhaps social capital. While it would be unlikely, as Seiter argues, for these to be translated into symbolic capital (except for situations where participants may decide to pursue a career in media or academics), what is important here is the degree of self-awareness among participants about the importance of such capital (even if it is not named as such). This self-awareness is expressed particularly in relation to television and globalization, as the following examples show:

> Edutainment is becoming important now with all the channels coming up. Lots of channels coming up, lots of channels. There are few channels catering to basic education part and few channels catering to basic entertainment part. So when you club these two in India, a man who is having at least a cable connection and a remote with him surfs like anything from one to the other. (Vijay)

> In general we are getting a chance to see how they [other countries] are currently doing things. We are getting the opportunity. There's a chance for us to pick up on the general knowledge, and realize that we also desire some changes. (Venkatesh) (translated from Telugu)

Television in general is thus seen as an opportunity for learning, motivation, and advancement. Along with some of the participants' comments on globalization, it would seem that there is a sense, in and about contemporary middle-class experience in India, of things opening up, and providing more knowledge. This is seen perhaps as both an aspiration, and a requisite for success in the emerging global economy. It is also instructive that participants do not make a distinction between "useful" and "trivial" knowledges (as knowledge about television may sometimes be dismissed in everyday life). Instead, for one participant, even the absence of certainties in television constitutes a form of knowledge, echoing perhaps his own apprehensions of uncertainty in a time of rapid social and cultural change:

> The experimental part of our life has been given in the TV channels . . . Because you see the way the people make the ideas they get, they do not have a clear kind of picture, but they try it. So I say it is experimental . . . I think I can call the producer or director a scientist. (Samir)

These perceptions of television as an agent of knowledge and change, and their implicit aspirations of mobility and success, are also evident among some of the working-class participants. For them, television's potential usefulness appears not so much for themselves, but in the aspirations they have for their children—and the clear value they placed on the fact that their children were going to school (where, as it turned out, they all sang "Made in India" during their annual day celebrations). However, there may be some important differences in the way that those who are "in the know" and those who are not encounter knowledge on television because of the increasing self-consciousness with which being "in the know" is itself celebrated, particularly on Channel V and MTV, and the growing necessity of being "in the know" in order to make sense of many music television programs.

Without certain kinds of knowledge, many of the pleasures and identifications of music television would be unavailable to audiences. However, what is unusual is that much of the pleasure in music television has also been made dependent by the nature of certain discourses on viewers' ability to recognize certain things, and in doing so, recognize themselves as being able to do that. For example, Channel V's frequent use of idiosyncratic English ("like this only") may be picked up by a lot of young viewers, but the full import of its self-consciousness and humor would lend itself only to those viewers whose English is so impeccable (and cultural capital so distinguished) that they would recognize "this only" as an Indian-English idiosyncracy (which they would never make the mistake of saying in a formal context). Sometimes, self-recognition is also tied up more explicitly with notions of distinction. Channel V's *Indian Top Ten* ("the only countdown that counts") promo begins by saying, "Throughout history, there are people who have said, while the rest have listened." The "rest" is what is perhaps needed for much of this self-consciousness to function.

In the light of some of these discourses, how would one characterize the position and relation of those participants in this study who are "in the know" to the "rest"? Although nothing that these participants said could be taken as an expression of self-perceived superiority, the fact that they understand certain discourses implies their engagement with them. In other words, even understanding the meaning of countdowns and *Made in India*, suggests that these participants respond at the level of intelligibility with what these discourses are saying. In particular, participants' belief that they are acting upon television as the "public," and upon the rest of the world as "Indians," show that they assume a certain kind of "authorial" role for themselves in these discourses. With their knowledge of music television, the ability to experience certain "pleasures of knowledge" (Corner, 1999), and consequently assume certain "authorial pleasures" (Fiske, 1987) as well, it would seem that these participants are indeed "in it," as the Channel V promo would say. However, does this kind of knowledge enable (and represent) the totality of their experience as a global television audience?

Another Knowledge

The knowledge that is employed in watching music television, however, extends beyond the self-conscious discourses of music television, drawing attention to the nature of the "lay epistemology" (Livingstone, 1999) that audiences bring to media texts. As I argued in Chapters 3 and 4, the reception of music countdowns and the *Made in India* video exceeded some of the inferences that could have been drawn from the texts alone—and the process of appropriation that I alluded to may be better understood here by examining how the "lay epistemology" that enabled a certain kind of reception entails not only familiarity with music television conventions and broader discourses about globalization and the nation, but also an emotional and relational sensibility that could carry epistemic significance as well.

In other words, it is important to note the presence of epistemic resources that enable the emphasis that participants—across the "in the know" gap—place on emotions and relationships. For instance, what sort of knowledge is being expressed when *Made in India* is described as being about "husbands"? Or, when one participant calls the Colonial Cousins' "Krishna" the only "meaningful song on television" because of its emotional representation of a troubled father-son relationship? Or even when, in the absence of knowledge about the name of the movie, song, or performer, a working-class participant refers to a song as "the one sung by a mother to her child"? One source for making sense of music television in terms of such emotional resonances and relational values is the long tradition entailed in the reception of Indian cinema. As Sara Dickey (1996) has shown in her ethnographic study of poor South Indian film viewers, the popular reception of Indian films is based on the making of "personal connections between (viewers) and their relationships . . . and the characters and the relationships shown on the screen" (p. 146). The melodramatic nature of Indian cinema, as she points out, is merely the form in which such identification can take place.

It is apparent in this study that emotional experience derived from relational narratives continues to be an important form of reception in India even in the age of music television. For some participants, those who are not "in the know," this is all there is to music television; not a countdown or a VJ, but simply a song with feeling, conveyed through music, lyrics, and acting. For the rest of the participants who are "in the know" and have indeed meaningfully engaged with the conventions of music television and the discourses of liberalization and globalization, music television is at its heart the expression of feelings about relations, but is *also* the world of countdowns and VJs. Rather than see these as two distinct forms of reception, it is more useful to examine the relative value of emotional and relational experiences, on the one hand, and the discursive claims about popularity, nationality, and globality, on the other. One way of approaching this question would be to take up the issue of "authorship" (McKinley, 1997) in audience research and examine the nature of the authority that participants implicitly or explicitly invoke in speaking about their reception experience.

The "in the know" participants *feel* music television as much as anyone else, but by the very fact of their being able to engage meaningfully with the new discourses are called upon to occupy certain subject positions in relation to these discourses. In other words, these participants assume their authority to speak as the "public" and as "Indians" in relation to these discourses. However, participants who have nothing else to speak from but their emotional and relational experience, all their implicit authority comes from these experiences alone. This is an implicit, unnamed form of assuming authority, similar to what Purnima Mankekar (1999) describes in her study as *bhaav* or meaning, suggesting a reception experience based on the process of . . ."surrender[ing] to the mood of what was being watched" (p. 25). If the key principle in deriving authority from emotional experience is one of "surrender," the stakes of seeking authority from the discourses of music television invoke a different movement altogether.

The discourses from which younger middle-class participants claim their authority call not so much on one's yielding to an emotional experience, but instead present a way of knowing that is modern, rational, and individually self-centered, marking the rise to prominence in Indian popular culture of what Sudipta Kaviraj (1992) in another context characterizes as "enumerated community" (as opposed to a "fuzzy community"). The discourses of enumeration by their very existence marginalize other forms of experience, or at least prevent these experiences from assuming epistemic authority. For example, the feelings in reception do not represent popularity on the countdown, but the expression of opinion does; either through cassette purchases, through letters, or through appearing before a microphone. The question, however, is whether there are indeed epistemic resources available for making sense of emotional and relational experiences outside the enumerative discourses of modernity.

Such a possibility exists in the traditional Indian theory of communication and performance known as *rasa*.[3] The central assumption of this theory, according to Owen Lynch (1990), is that "one's emotions are one's true self and the 'essence' of true reality" (p. 18). The modern, Western notion of the self, on the other hand, privileges rationality over emotionality and approaches emotions as irrational, natural (as opposed to cultural, or "civilized"), and passive. In other words, emotions are seen in Western modernity as things that happen when the "real" rational self breaks down. Another important distinction between the modern notion of the self and that embodied in the rasa theory is the former's emphasis on individuality and interiority. The emotional character of the self is not seen in rasa theory as an internal quality of the individual, but as something that arises because of the self's social and relational location.

According to the rasa theory, the emotional self cannot be separated from the rational self or the body either. For instance, the notion of *manassu,* used by at least one participant in the context of *Made in India,* implies both "mind" and "heart," in modern terms. Thus, according to this theory, reception would be seen not in terms of a primary denotative meaning and a secondary connotative meaning, but in terms of emotional and relational experience itself.

Thus, as Lewis Rowell (1992) writes, rasa may be seen as:

> A transcendent mode of emotional awareness by which all aspects of a performance are integrated, an awareness that rises above the circumstances that awakened it . . . and generalizes the individual emotional states of the spectators into a single emotional field. (p. 328)

Emotional experience is thus seen not as a secondary, individual state, but as the level at which reception takes place as a *social experience*. From such a perspective, media representations can be seen not in the modern-Western notion of having to re-present a preexistent reality, but instead as something that heightens the emotional experiences of audiences and consequently enables them to experience their true identity—which is social and emotional rather than individual and rational. Such a notion is explicitly in evidence in some of the statements made by participants in this study in relation to *Made in India*. This video is seen as a representation of a feeling that is then labeled as "Indian," and again, importantly, this is not the evocation of an individual sense of feeling, but one that arises in relational terms ("husbands," for example). Claims about "true identity," however, raise immediate questions about what the role of such a perspective could be in the present context. Without recourse to "nativism," it is, I believe, possible and important to examine what this episteme—the sensibilities of which are very much evident in modern media audiences—implies for the imagination of a globality that expresses its nonmodernity both resistively and engagingly with modernity, and is universalist and anti-imperialist.

Another Globality

Even an attempt to begin an alternative imagining of globality on this basis requires an acknowledgment of the constraints placed upon it by the tyranny of modernity. One of the key mechanisms with which modernity asserts its epistemic privilege is by positing itself in opposition to something called "tradition." Tradition may be either reviled as something to be overcome (as in the case of the modernization paradigm into which much of the world was goaded after decolonization), yearned for as something originary and pristine (especially when the West looks to the "East"), or sanctified as a revanchist goal (in most modern fundamentalisms). The preeminence of modernity circumscribes what tradition could be in the first place. As Anthony Giddens (1990) points out, "Tradition can only be justified in the light of knowledge which is not itself authenticated by tradition" (p. 38). In other words, tradition is something that is defined as such on the terms of modernity, even as it is reinvented from one generation to another. An epistemic alternative to modernity however, needs to begin not with the notion of tradition, but by drawing from what Giddens calls the premodern. Is there something in the premodern that could inform contemporary globality?

The apparent temporal contradiction in these terms may be worked out by situating this question in the broader question of universalism. The "global" and "universal" (Tagg, 1997; Waters, 1995) are both connected to the history of Western imperialism and the worldwide advent of capitalism and modernity. However, does this imply, as one recent visionary of this world-order has argued (Huntington, 1993), that only the West is capable of universalism while all the other "civilizations" are doomed to their narrow particularisms? Is globality doomed to be Western—and imperialist? Huntington's millennially correct manifesto (he does acknowledge that the other is civilized as well) represents what may be described as an imperial globality. Its presumptuous univocality and ethnocentrism have been clearly challenged in a number of scholarly interventions, most notably in the context of the "liberalism" of Asian modernities by Aihwa Ong (1999).

However, a distinctly nonmodern universalism that would challenge Huntington and imperial globality may be found in Ashis Nandy's (1987) reading of Gandhi. Nandy writes that Gandhi was no cultural relativist in the modern sense of the word. Instead, he believed in the universality of cultures, and saw only modernity as dividing the West from its colonial victims and also from its own humanity. The most instructive insight one could draw here from Gandhi's politico-religious opposition to modernity is his critique of the evacuation of accountability from social relations, a condition that Nandy characterizes as "technocracy." The key feature of technocracy as a system of power under modernity is the elevation to truth of a knowledge based on the suppression of emotions and ethics—even as these are supposed to promote noble ideals like "equality." Gandhi's critique of modernity, according to Nandy (1987), came not from such a rational, instrumental definition of knowledge, and its attendant notions of cultural "difference," but from a profound and nonmodern understanding of the notion of "equality":

> Equality for him . . . was ultimately the mutuality and nurture one could provide another, not in return for or in exchange of what the other had done for one but in "equitable return" for the over-all nurture one had received from the human and non-human cosmos. (p. 151)

The notion of overall nurture here suggests the presence of social obligation not only as a guiding principle for nature and society but also as a scaffold for a certain kind of subjectivity as well, emphasizing the relatedness of individuals and the claims of belonging upon each other in which they live, as opposed to the modern, Western notion of the autonomous, self-interested individual. While the notion of obligation emphasizes, in a manner of speaking, who one ought to be in "'equitable return' for the over-all nurture one ha[s] received," its root in the Sanskrit word "Adhikara" also suggests authority gained through the enactment of one's obligations (Mishra, 1998). While the importance of such authority for identity in interpersonal and familial relations in India (Vaidyanathan, 1989) and the role of "obligation" in modern political and social development (Rudolph & Rudolph, 1967) has been noted, what is relevant here is the emphasis these concepts place on mutuality and accountability in social identities and relations, and the broader universal vision that could derive from it.

It is my contention that such a globality, based on relational authority and emotional subjectivity, coexists with the modern, imperial, discursive form of globality in the Indian music television audience. If the latter deals with "what the world means" expressed as territoriality, control, and individuality, the former derives from "what means the world" in terms of the longings and belongings that constitute the intensities of everyday life and interpersonal interaction (Juluri, 1999). Becoming a global audience, as this study tells us, is but a moment of self-reflection along what seems like an inexorable historic passage; for the generational inscription of this passage is all too evident.

The young, global-looking, Indian-feeling music television audience is, at one level, the outcome of an ingenious marketing experiment that has produced a complex form of hegemony indeed. On the one hand, this is a transnational form of hegemony that entails a transformation of India's global self-perception from anticolonial struggle, Third World solidarity, and eminence in the Non-Aligned Movement to an imagined self-congratulatory status as an emerging economic, scientific, military, and cultural superpower. On the other hand, this is also a transgenerational form of hegemony that has surreptitiously gained the consent of parents and children for the latter's cooptation—they can be cynical, individualistic, and materialistic (as the survey quoted at the beginning of this chapter says), but it would all be welcomed as the great Indian tradition if they wear an "I love India" T-shirt and go to a temple.

Such a characterization seems harsh, especially in the context of the obvious cordiality of the people who participated in these interviews. This is one example perhaps of how the broad disjuncture between "audiences" and "people" plays out. I would be inclined to say that as people, and considering exactly what they said, they could be the agents of an alternative globality; but as "audiences," also considering what they said, they are a part of what could be described as a hegemonic globality, a view of the world at the intersection of the alternative globality from which they have come and the imperial globality into which they have been hurled. The future for them will be one of perhaps greater globalization than for generations before—migrations, media, relationships, fragmentations, as yet unimaginable cohesions and communities. However, for the children of the 1990s who came in to an India of satellite television and gated compounds, and cities without air and sky, the experience would perhaps be even more intense.

Stuart Hall (1997) jokes that the "organic community" is something a lot of people think they had in their childhood. If successive generations seem to feel that way, then perhaps it is not just nostalgia, but a sign that things are getting worse. One example that may be useful here pertains to the transformation of the mythological Indian film. In my childhood, these were still popular, and on the edge of being wiped out by the "angry young man" vigilante films of the 1970s. I remember two Telugu films here. *Yasodha-Krishna*, a retelling of the popular story of Krishna as a child, although the emphasis in this film is on the maternal bonds that existed between the boy-avatar and his mother across multiple incarnations. The other one was called *Vinayaka Vijayam*, the story of the elephant-headed God Vinayaka (also known as Ganesha). In one scene, Vinayaka and his brother Murugan decide to have a friendly race around the world. Being a

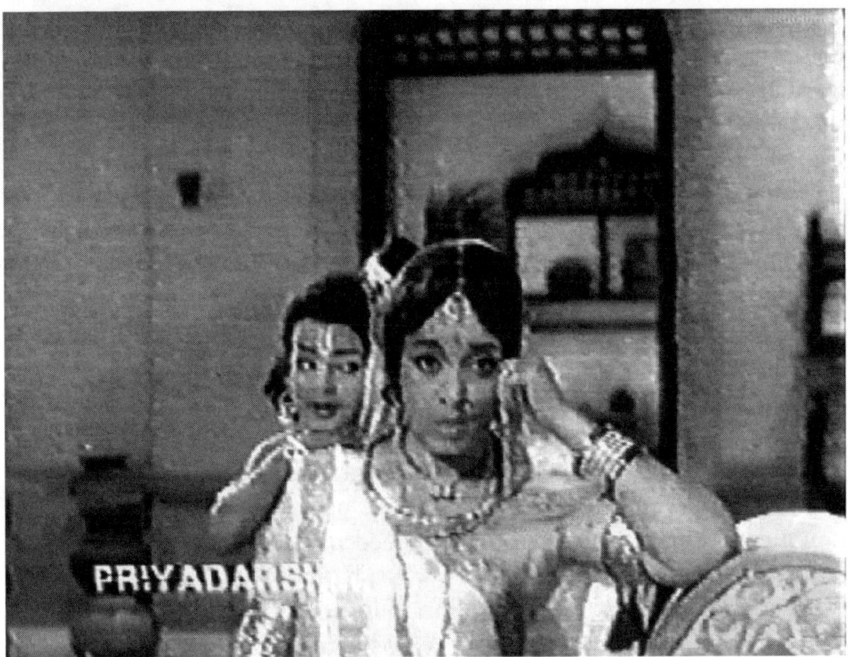

FIGURE 9 The child-god Krishna endears himself to his mother Yasodha in the Telugu film Yasodha-Krishna. Baby Sridevi as Krishna and Jamuna as Yasodha.

spry boy-god with a peacock as his *vaahana* (vehicle), Murugan sets off into outer space. Being elephant-headed and stuck with only a mouse to ride on, Vinayaka wisely circumambulates Shiva and Parvathi instead. Vinayaka wins.

These "religious" films, like many of the social melodramas of postindependence Indian cinema, offered not only an intensely nonmodern form of representation and reception (Das Gupta, 1989; Eck, 1981) but moral solutions and ethical goals to the relational problems of everyday life as well (Chakravarty 1993). In other words, mythological films were all about a popular sentiment pertaining to family and relationships that was expressed and embodied in divine images and stories. By the 1980s, however, mythologicals had completely disappeared from cinema, but reappeared instead in serialized form in Hindi on national television. The centralized homogenization through television of what had been a fairly heterogeneous and regionalized tradition and its implication in the subsequent rise of modernized and militarized interpretations of religion are now well known. In the 1990s, I saw Krishna and Vinayaka once again, on music television. Once on a Channel V promo I saw an actor painted blue and wearing costume jewelry, and thought he was supposed to be Krishna. I also thought in an old-fashioned way that it was another example of the cultural plundering of India. Another time, a Tamil pop music video showed young boys and girls dancing near waterfalls with Ganesha paper-masks chanting, "In the name of you, we start the day."

These examples of religion in the popular Indian consciousness embody some of the consequences of what becoming a global audience has entailed. A popular sentiment that has had the strongest sense of humanity at its heart and worked its silent and dignified way through ages of conquest, colonization, and modernizations now attempts to face itself once again in and through a medium (satellite television) that is perhaps only less astounding in its magnitude than the madness of the social reconfigurations that surround it (globalization). In other words, in all the complexity of its coalitions and contradictions, the Indian global audience is fundamentally an aspiration to resecure a place on what hitherto was unnoticed, but quite always there, the bedrock of "emotions" and "relations" that is now slipshod and somewhat shattered, too.

The main location for this aspiration is indeed in the media, and if an alternative globality based on it is ever to be imagined—as much as recognized—the mandate of media studies becomes so much more important. The territorial ambitions of globalization, and its implication in growing complex and distant social relations to which we can hardly begin to give meaning, have made media globalities an everyday reality. These media globalities, whether in terms of institutional imperatives or failures of imagination, mostly derive from and also promote what Edward Said (1978) has elsewhere identified as a "textual attitude." The complexities of our global situatedness may make such an attitude impossible to avoid, but what can indeed be contested is the "restorative citation of antecedent authority" (p. 176) that media discourses entail; or, to paraphrase Hall (1992), keep those "old movies" from getting made. Orientalism is now everywhere.

Audience researchers are qualified to advance such a mission. Seiter (1999) has pointed out the need to "challenge the claim that people [only] want what they already have on television" (p. 132). In the case of this study, it seems that what people want from television is not necessarily what they see on it, but is something that may be suggested by the nobility of their aspirations in the meanings they constructed around what is at best an attractive but culturally impoverished and socially undesirable set of representations for the intense and complex experiences that they are living every day under globalization. To put it another way, India's music-television generation, which came of age in the 1990s, has encountered

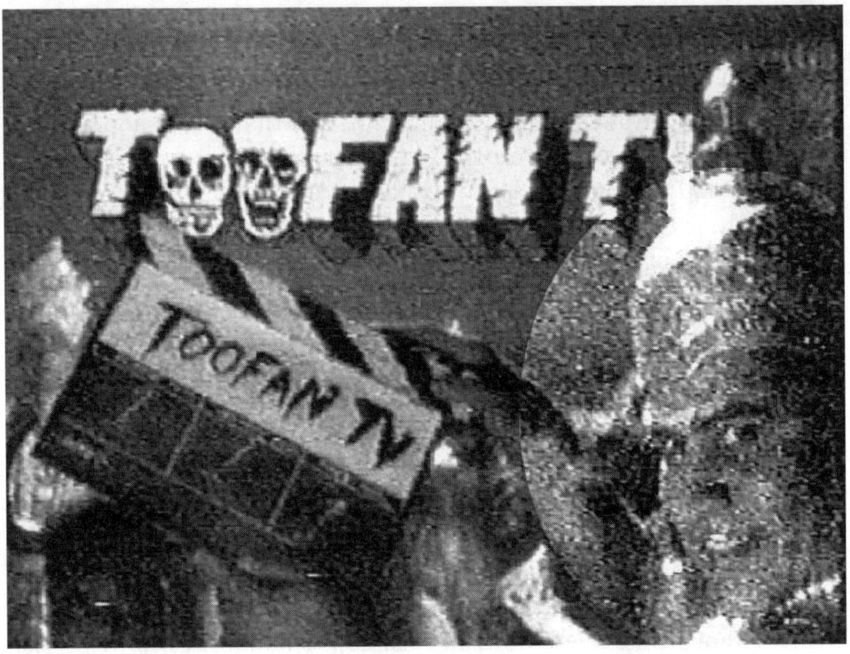

FIGURE 10 Krishna, the exotic extra, fades into a weird mélange of demons and savages in this promo for a Channel V program on Indian horror cinema.

another curious and cruel twist of social history—that of having to define itself and its aspirations in relation to media representations that are not the resources for self-reflection they or their elders think they are.

One form of survival under colonialism, as Nandy (1983) points out, has been the ability to avoid or resist definition in the terms of modernity. However, the terms of modernity are no longer administered only from dusty punkah-flapping colonial bungalows, but in the homes and hearts of ordinary people as well, and this is where a politics of definition is being confronted. Globalization, for the television audience, is perhaps understood as a call to define one's self in a new global context that is real in the complexity of its interdependencies and relations and also imagined in its meanings and values. At the core of this process is a condition that is perhaps as global as the planetary plagues that afflict our time in history. The condition is indeed the sentiment—the totality of one's life that exists beyond and in spite of the physical and mental blinders imposed on one's self by the social conditions and cultural ideologies of modernity. The sentiment is by no means exclusively Indian; in fact there is more than one expression for it in India as well. For example, the three leading film industries in India, Hindi, Tamil, and Telugu, all have their own idiomatic way of dealing with it and struggling for it. The results range from the sublimely sentimental to the grotesque, but it would seem that every conceivable human condition has an Indian film song to deal with it (and the seemingly inconceivable, or unhuman are perhaps best dealt with on Jerry Springer and Fox News).

In all these cases, though, what is at stake is the struggle to preserve a sentiment through change and appropriate reinvention as it passes from generation to generation. In the context of present-day globalization, this struggle also acquires a market-inflected transnational form. Indians would like to be recognized, and music television seems to be doing this at various levels—at the level of the unnamed sentimentality that is invisible and pervasive as nature; and at the new imagined level of nations and territories. This desire for recognition perhaps comes from the fact that the universality of sentimentality is seen more clearly by those whose worlds have not yet been convoluted completely by modernity than by those who inhabit an advanced modernity that may deny them an understanding of the true conditions of their existence in terms of "emotions and "relations," although these emotions and relations could just as easily be seen as the foundation of advanced modernity as well, even if their existence is possible only in peculiarly rationalized forms. In other words, it is not difficult for the Indian audience to think of the family as a universal sentiment; but if it has to define itself exclusively because that is the only way in which it can engage with the terms of definition set by the West, it will do so. The terms on which recognition is bartered are of course highly unequal and counternatural, and serve to appropriate, as I have argued in this book, the nobility of sentiment into hard and hollow labels of "identity" that are strangely premised on "difference." The lesson that can be applied from the globalization of the Indian audience to the predilection of the global audience in general is perhaps just this: How can the world know itself to be universal, sentimental, and mutually accountable when the massive machinery of media and modernity that can technologically facilitate such a possibility represents the historic antithesis to such a world?

One modest answer to this question is the possibility that the struggle over the sentiment can demand new forms of representation and recognition, and ultimately new conditions for the continued existence of this sentiment. In other words, one critique and prescription that could be advanced would have to focus on the creative and imaginative capacities of media themselves. Could the media, in various forms and contexts, acquire a different way of representing globalities? The longing that pervades the reception of Indian music television is perhaps for such representations, and the possibility that these representations, with all the mighty forces of mass mediation behind them will manifest as social change—and preservation in some way. To summarize the historical specificities of this desire, one can simply look at the last decade. Amidst social upheavals and family fragmentations, we watched our film songs and music videos and wore our pennants of family pride high. Our ground is stolen, but our feet are now imposed in strange vectors in the skies. Our lives are roller-coasters for solo riders. We are learning the bang of the thrill from the thrill-seeking West, and we have suddenly turned to what it is we are losing and with a fervent hope against history we hope to save it by advertising our family and our culture to the world. Perhaps one can even rise above the fact that Hindu Gods (noncopyrighted) are sold in hippy stalls on Telegraph Avenue in Berkeley (and, more egregiously, by the meat section in an upscale grocery store there, too). Somewhere in the Indian imagination, though, the Gods are still singing and dancing with their families and friends, with the promise of new practices and understandings of world, self, and family that can sustain a sentiment rooted in mutuality and accountability as a global condition.

APPENDIX A

PROFILE OF INTERVIEW GROUP PARTICIPANTS

Group	Name[a]	Gender	Age/Status	Class[b]	Channels[c]
1	Mamatha	F	High school	M	E, H, T
	Nisha	F	High school	M	H
	Maya	F	High school	M	E, H
	Kartika	F	High school	M	H
2	Alpana	F	Undergraduate	M	E
	Deepika	F	Undergraduate	M	E, H
	Anila	F	Graduate	M	E
	Pratibha	F	Undergraduate	M	E, H
	Sonia	F	Undergraduate	M	E, H
	Ayesha	F	Undergraduate	M	E, H
3	Radhika	F	Undergraduate	M	E, H
	Padma	F	Undergraduate	M	H, E
	Arun	M	Undergraduate	M	E
4	Anjali	F	Graduate	M	T, H
	Kamala	F	Graduate	M	T, H
	Jyothi	F	Graduate	M	T, H
	Lakshmi	F	Graduate	W	T, H
5	Murali	M	Graduate	M	T
	Mohan	M	Graduate	W	E, H (DD)[d]
	Ramesh	M	Graduate	W	E, T
	Kiran	M	Graduate	M	E, H, T
	Raja	M	Graduate	M	T
6	Pragathi	F	Junior high	W	T, H, E
	Ajay	M	High school	W	H, T, E
	Dinesh	M	High school	M	H
	Sarala	F	High school	M	T, H, E

(continued)

(continued)

Group	Name[a]	Gender	Age/Status	Class[b]	Channels[c]
7	Vinod	M	Middle school	W	T
	Sailesh	M	Primary school	W	T
	Shekhar	M	Primary school	W	T
	Amala	F	Domestic worker	W	T
	Durga	F	Domestic worker	W	T
8	Bhanu	F	Research scholar	M	E, H
	Vijay	M	Research scholar	M	E, H
	Naresh	M	Research scholar	M	E, H
	Venkatesh	M	Research scholar	M	T, E
	Gopal	M	Lab Assistant	M	T, E (sports)[e]
	Sandhya	F	Govt. Employee	M	T (DD)
9	Hussain	M	Service	M	H
	Rashid	M	Overseas service	M	H, E (news)[f]
	Praveen	M	Research scholar	M	E
	Jaya	F	Teacher	M	H, T (DD)
	Samir	M	Teacher	M	H (DD)

Note. Sample size = 42 participants in nine groups. Female participants numbered 22 while male participants numbered 20.

a. Names have been altered to protect identities of participants.

b. *M* indicates middle class while *W* indicates working class.

c. Channels viewed listed by language of channel programming. E indicates English; H indicates Hindi; T indicates Telugu. Channels also listed in order of language preference. English channel viewers have access to global programming; Hindi channel viewers have access to national programming; Telugu channel viewers have access to regional programming.

d. DD indicates that participant has access only to national terrestrial network Doordarshan and not satellite/cable television.

e. Indicates that English channels are only viewed for sports programming.

f. Indicates that English channels are only viewed for news programming.

APPENDIX B

MUSIC COUNTDOWN SHOWS IN HYDERABAD (1997)

Channel	Show[a]	Language/Format[b]
Asianet	Anchor Best 10	Malayalam, Film
ATN	Blast Off	Hindi, Film
	Stardust Hot 20	Hindi, Film
Doordarshan	All the Best	Hindi, Film
	Ek Se Badkar Ek	Hindi, Film
	Superhit Muqabla	Hindi, Film
EL	Hey Ho Ha	Hindi, Film
	Public Demand	Hindi, Film
	The Real Countdown	Hindi, Pop
	Superhit Hungama	Hindi, Film
	Top of the Tops	Hindi, Film
ETV	Rin Priyaragalu	Telugu, Film
Gemini	Santoor Top 10	Telugu, Film
Home	Hit Hit Hooray	Hindi, Film
	Popularly Yours	Hindi, Film
MTV	Asia Hitlist	International, Pop
	Europe Top 20	International, Pop
	India Hit List	Hindi/International, Pop
	US Top 20	International, Pop
Sony	Chicklets Take 5	Hindi, Pop
	Hum Aapke Hain Kountdown	Hindi, Film
Star Plus	Ooh La La	Hindi, Film
Sun	Philips Super 10	Tamil, Film
V	Asian Top 20	International, Pop
	Billboard US Top 20	International, Pop
	BPL Oye	Hindi, Film
	Indian Top 10	Hindi/International, Pop
	Top of the Pops	International, Pop
	V-1s	International, Pop

(continued)

(continued)

Channel	Show[a]	Language/Format[b]
Z	Philips Top 10	Hindi, Film
Z Cinema	Ikka pe Ikka	Hindi, Film

a. Show names are often inseparable from company/brand sponsor names.

b. Language and genre. (E=English; H=Hindi; T=Telugu.) Presentation varies.

NOTES

Introduction

1. Literally means "the letter at the end." The game in its simplest form consists of people singing songs that begin with the same syllable that the earlier song has ended on. The TV version has further variations, and the program has remained among India's most popular cable and satellite shows since the mid-1990s.
2. I use the terms "normalization" and "naturalization" in this book somewhat interchangeably. My aim is not necessarily to embark on a strict Foucaltian analysis of institutional practices and discourses, but to instead draw attention to the fact that ". . . meanings that are socially, historically, economically, and culturally determined . . . are 'experienced' as natural [or] inevitable, timeless, universal, genetic (and hence unarguable)" (O'Sullivan, Hartley, Saunders, & Fiske, 1983, 143).
3. The semiotic implications of "flows," as discussed by Jensen (1995), are particularly relevant in the case of music television. Viewing music television programs, including countdowns, rarely seems to be a bounded activity. It is worth stressing the fact that viewers may switch frequently, but certain music videos and film songs remain pervasive—the same song could appear in multiple countdowns, in non-countdown music programs, in programs about films, and in advertisements for cassettes and films. Audience negotiation of flow is also seen as being especially useful for music television programming, for this is where viewers often turn to from other channels, according to MTV Asia CEO Tom Freston (Pinto, 1997).
4. Prior to 1991, perhaps the only well-known countdown-based music program in India was not on television but on radio. *Binaca Geet Mala*, which was broadcast on Radio Ceylon under the anchorship of Amin Sayani, played Hindi film songs.
5. One of the music retailers I interviewed was especially upset by this, and felt that the music companies' representatives who came from Mumbai did not adequately pursue retailers in Hyderabad.

Chapter 1
The Commercial Context of Music Television in India

1. Five paise (0.125 cents) is about what media planners assess as a fair price from television networks for an average television viewer in India (Sahai, 1997).

2. Star TV (Satellite Television Asian Region) initially broadcast to China and Taiwan, and later extended its scope to India and most of Asia. Its initial broadcasts to India featured mainly Western programming like soap operas and music videos. It was acquired by News Corporation soon after (Shah, 1997).
3. At the time of this study, my cable provider flashed the following message after an overnight interruption: "Antisocial elements had cut off our cable wire. We condemn this timid act by our competitors."
4. Some of the proposals of this Bill include limiting foreign equity in media ventures to 49%, requiring mandatory uplinking from India for broadcasters, and certain cross-media ownership restrictions (Chatterjee, 1997 June 18). However, a more recent policy announcement made important changes in terms of opening up Indian film and print business to foreign ownership (2002).
5. This relationship is occasionally challenged, as seen for instance in the news report that TV crews were denied entry into a Hyderabad film studio because they had not paid an "entry fee" (Rao, 1997).
6. Television Rating Points (TRPs) have become the new currency for the television-advertiser exchange, although there has been a dispute between the "official" ratings provider and the one that stole the lead in installing Peoplemeters in various cities. The somewhat blind rush towards TRPs has had at least some producers lamenting the days when ". . . people used to judge the popularity of the serials by the deserted roads" (quoted in Hassan, 1997, August 8–14).
7. Even as the new multichannel environment has necessitated a conscious investment in establishing individual brand identities for channels, often through creative use of promos (Kohli, 1997), an interesting practice has been the explicit branding of programs to complement their sponsors' products (Chaya, 1997). Product names are routinely incorporated into program titles, and especially in the case of music countdowns, the only way to even distinguish one "top ten" from another would be by mentioning the sponsor's name. For instance, the statement "I saw Top Ten last night" would be meaningless unless one specified whether this was Philips Top Ten or Santoor Top Ten and so on.
8. Arathoon (1997) describes 1997 as the year the "bubble burst for advertising," when a 30 percent growth rate dropped to about half. Around the same time, MNC's share of advertising expenditure grew to nearly 60%. For MNC's, the once fabled Indian middle-class market was proving to be a "Waterloo" in the words of Annuncio (1997). The middle classes were not 250 million strong as originally thought, and they simply did not have the kind of purchasing power global brands demanded.
9. Sony has also announced plans to enter film music. While it does not intend to produce feature films, it has tied up with Rajshri Films to make a "film-like non-film music video" (Mukherjee, 1997, July 15–21).
10. The nonresident Indian market is an important one as well. See Ray and Jacka (1996) and Yadava (1999) for a discussion of Indian media exports.
11. A more recent estimate by Arthur Anderson consultants put the total number of TV households at 79.4 million and cable and satellite (C/S) households at 37 million (Elsham, 2002 March 22).
12. In this context, the cable-operated channels are becoming increasingly important for advertisers not only because they are bound to be provided in the main line-up

for subscribers, but also because there are less legal restrictions for these channels to show the latest Indian film releases (Mukherjee, 1998).

Chapter 2
Music Television and Its Audiences

1. For a useful discussion of the demographic distribution of taste in popular music, albeit in a different context from that of this study, see Shepherd (1986).
2. The political nature of the boundaries that separate music from noise is further explored by Jacques Attali (1985), who situates these boundaries in the broader political economy of capitalism. While Attali's work may overstate the importance of music as an agent of history, it is nonetheless useful in recognizing the fact that music, or the organization of sound that is recognizable as music, is a powerful form for the construction and maintenance of community, and music itself is seen by Attali as a form in which power links its centers to its dispersed subjects.
3. Music television producers are invested in the notion of "attitude" as well, and define it as "aggressive self-awareness." There is also a perception among media executives that fashions and "attitudes" in India follow a top-down path in class terms, while in the West these are often lifted from the street styles of less privileged groups (Hussain, 1999, February 10–16).
4. "Overacting," or simply, "O.A.," is a part of Telugu youth slang as well, often used to tell someone to calm down.
5. I found a pervasive and grotesque example of this during my visits in India—very young boys doing a dance move from Indian film songs which is often called the "pelvic thrust." Although this looks rather vulgar, parents, it appears, try to pass this off as something "cute."
6. A marketing study sponsored by MTV found that 69 percent of young people believe that a song's popularity depends on its visuals (Mukherjee, 1997).

Chapter 3
Liberalization and the Public

1. It is worth mentioning here that at the time of writing, the biggest television phenomenon in India is the quiz show *Kaun Banega Crorepati (Who'll become a Crorepati)*. One crore is 10 million rupees or about a quarter of a million dollars. Another program now offers ten times that amount for winning a singing contest (Chougule, 2000).
2. This is the exact word used by Channel V's Jules Fuller in describing the channel's marketing and programming strategy (Hussain, 1997).
3. A pun on "Door" (distant) in Doordarshan (which literally means "watching from afar").
4. Only one group of participants had been on television. They said that MTV had come to record an episode of one its college shows on their campus and complained that they were told what songs to dedicate.

5. The autorickshaw is another favorite symbol of music television's self-exoticization. Channel V once offered a ride in an auto as the prize for one of its contests.

Chapter 4
Globalization and the Nation

1. "Vande Mataram," meaning "salutations to the motherland" is India's national song (the national anthem is "Jana Gana Mana"). This nationalistic Bengali song and the slogan "Vande Mataram" were an important part of India's freedom struggle.
2. While the city of Bangalore, in the neighboring state of Karnataka is one of the first Indian cities with a major software-export base, Hyderabad has rapidly become an important center as well (Iyer, 1997). This is not in the least due to the agenda of Andhra Pradesh's "Laptop" Chief Minister, Chandrababu Naidu, whose recent accomplishments include getting President Clinton to visit Hyderabad in early 2000 and praise his contributions toward the information technology sector.
3. For instance, Aerosmith's Nine Lives album featured on its cover a famous image of Krishna atop a sea serpent, but with his head replaced by that of a cat's. This may have been just exotic to Western consumers, but to at least the Hindu group which protested and got Sony to change the cover, it meant more ("Sony accused . . . ," 1997).
4. Butcher's critique, and one that is relevant here, focuses on the images used to represent India as a spectacle ostensibly for global consumption; effectively turning India, in the eyes of the West, from "an incomprehensible mystery" to a "bite-sized biscuit"; from orientalism to globalism, as it were.

Chapter 5
Becoming a Global Audience

1. From a 1997 survey conducted by advertising agency Ogilvy and Mather (O&M) which proposed the name "Genie Generation" (Generation who Independently Engage in Society) for young postliberalization Indians (Ghose & Jahagirdar, 1998).
2. The structured interview and video screening worked with most participants, but was perhaps a little alien for those who would have perhaps preferred a more open-ended conversation (into which questions about music television could have been inserted).
3. While this theory is usually understood as a set of codes for traditional performance, what it underscores is a premodern Indian worldview that situates emotional experience in the context of interrelated notions of body, space, knowledge, and representation. Rasa literally means "juice," and the use of metaphors of food to describe emotional experience is not uncommon in premodern philosophy. The body, in its physical and emotional aspects, is seen as nothing but the product of food. Food, in turn, refers not only to actual food, but anything that is consumed, including artistic performance. See Rowell (1992) for a comprehensive discussion.

REFERENCES

Academic Sources

Anderson, B. (1991). *Imagined communities: Reflections on the origins and spread of nationalism*. London: Verso.

Ang, I. (1996). *Living room wars: Rethinking media audiences for a postmodern world.* New York: Routledge.

Ang, I. (1991). *Desperately seeking the audience*. New York: Routledge.

Ang, I. (1990). Culture and communication: Towards an ethnographic critique of media consumption in the transnational system. *European Journal of Communication*, 5, 239–60.

Appadurai, A. (1990). Disjuncture and difference in the global cultural economy. *Public Culture*, 2, 2, 1–24.

Appadurai, A., & Breckenridge, C. (1996). Public modernity in India. In C. Breckenridge (Ed.). *Consuming modernity: Public culture in a South Asian world* (pp. 1–16). Minneapolis: University of Minnesota Press.

Ashcroft, B., Griffiths, G., & Tiffin, H. (1998). *Key concepts in postcolonial studies.* New York: Routledge.

Attali, J. (1985). *Noise: The political economy of music* (B. Massumi, Trans.). Minneapolis: University of Minnesota Press.

Austin, J., & Willard, M. (1998). *Generations of youth: Youth cultures and history in twentieth century America*. New York: New York University Press.

Banks, J. (1996). *Monopoly television: MTV's quest to control the music*. Boulder, CO: Westview.

Berland, J. (1993). Sound, image and social space: Music video and media reconstruction. In S. Frith, A. Goodwin, & L. Grossberg (Eds.). *Sound and Vision: The music video reader* (pp. 25–43). New York: Routledge.

Bourdieu, P. (1984). *Distinction: A social critique of the judgment of taste* (R. Nice, Trans.). Cambridge, MA: Harvard University Press.

Buell, F. (1994). *National culture and the new global system*. Baltimore, MD: Johns Hopkins University Press.

Burnett, R. (1996). *The global jukebox: The international music industry*. New York: Routledge.

Butcher, M. (1999). Parallel texts: The body and television in India. In C. Brosius & M. Butcher (Eds.). *Image journeys: Audio-visual media and cultural change in India* (pp. 165–198). New Delhi: Sage.

Butcher, M. (1997). Looking at Miss World. *Seminar*, 453, 16–20.

Chadha, K., & Kavoori, A. (2000). Media imperialism revisited: Some findings from the Asian case. *Media, Culture, and Society*, 22, 415–432.

Chakravarty, S. (1993). *National identity in Indian popular cinema 1947–1987*. Austin: University of Texas Press.

Chen, K. (1998). Introduction: The decolonization question. In K. Chen (Ed.). *Trajectories: InterAsia cultural studies* (pp. 1–53). New York: Routledge.

Corner, J. (1999). *Critical ideas in television studies*. New York: Oxford University Press.

Curtin, M. (1999). Feminine desire in the age of satellite television. *Journal of Communication*, *49*, 55–69.

Das Gupta, C. (1989). Seeing and believing, science and mythology: Notes on the "mythological" genre. *Film Quarterly*, 42, 12–18.

Davies, M., Nandy, A., & Sardar, Z. (1993). *Barbaric others: A manifesto on Western racism*. London: Pluto.

Dickey, S. (1996). Consuming utopia: Film watching in Tamil Nadu. In C. Breckenridge (Ed.). *Consuming modernity: Public culture in a South Asian world* (pp. 131–155). Minneapolis: University of Minnesota Press.

Eck, D. (1981). *Darsan: Seeing the divine image in India*. New York: Columbia University Press.

Farrell, G. (1997). *Indian music and the west.* Oxford: Clarendon.

Ferguson, M. (1992). The mythology about globalization. *European Journal of Communication*, 7, 69–93.

Fernandes, L. (2000). Nationalizing the "global": Media images, cultural politics and the middle class in India. *Media, Culture, and Society*, 22, 611–628.

Feuer, J. (1992). Genre study and television. In R. Allen (Ed.). *Channels of discourse, reassembled* (pp. 138–59). Chapel Hill, NC: University of North Carolina Press.

Fiske, J. (1987). *Television culture*. New York: Routledge.

Frith, S. (1996). *Performing rites: On the value of popular music*. Cambridge, MA: Harvard University Press.

Ganguly, K. (1992). Accounting for others: Feminism and representation. In L. Rakow (Ed.). *Women making meaning: New feminist directions in communication* (pp. 60–79). New York: Routledge.

Gaonkar, D. (1999). On alternative modernities. *Public Culture*, *11*, 1, 1–18.

Garnham, N. (1995). Political economy and cultural studies: Reconciliation or divorce? *Critical Studies in Mass Communication*, *12*, 64–71.

Gibson, T. (2000). Beyond cultural populism: Notes toward the critical ethnography of media audiences. *Journal of Communication Inquiry*, *24*, 253–76.

Giddens, A. (1990). *The consequences of modernity*. Stanford, CA: Stanford University Press.

Goodwin, A. (1992). *Dancing in the distraction factory: Music television and popular culture*. Minneapolis: University of Minnesota Press.

Grossberg, L. (1997). *Dancing in spite of myself: Essays on popular culture*. Durham, NC: Duke University Press.

Grossberg, L. (1995). Cultural studies vs. political economy: Is anybody else bored with this debate? *Critical Studies in Mass Communication, 12*, 72–81.

Hall, S. (1997). Old and new identities, old and new ethnicities. In A. King (Ed.). *Culture, globalization and the world system: Contemporary conditions for the representation of identity* (pp. 41–67). Minneapolis: University of Minnesota Press.

Hall, S. (1992). Race, culture and communication: Looking backward and forward at cultural studies. *Rethinking Marxism*, 5, 1, 11–18.

Hall, S. (1986). The problem of ideology: Marxism without guarantees. *Journal of Communication Inquiry, 10*, 5–27.

Hall, S. (1982). The rediscovery of ideology: Return of the repressed in media studies. In M. Gurevitch, T. Bennett, J. Curran, & S. Woollacott (Eds.). *Culture, society, and the media* (pp. 56–90). London: Methuen.

Hall, S. (1993). Encoding, decoding. In S. During (Ed.). *The cultural studies reader* (pp. 90–103). New York: Routledge. Originally published in 1973.

Hartley, J. (1992). *The politics of pictures: The creation of the public in the age of popular media*. New York: Routledge.

Hay, J. (1996). Afterword: The place of the audience: Beyond audience studies. In J. Hay, L. Grossberg, & E. Wartella (Eds.). *The audience and its landscape* (pp. 359–78). Boulder, CO: Westview.

Herman, E., & McChesney, R. (1997). *The global media: The new missionaries of global capitalism*. Washington, DC: Cassell.

Huntington, S. (1993). The clash of civilizations? *Foreign Affairs, 3*, 22–49.

Jenks, C. (Ed.). (1995). *Visual culture*. New York: Routledge.

Jensen, K. (1995). *The social semiotics of mass communication*. Thousand Oaks, CA: Sage.

Juluri, V. (1999). Global weds local: The reception of *Hum aapke hain koun*. *European Journal of Cultural Studies*, 2, 2, 231–48.

Juluri, V. (1998a). Globalizing audience studies: The audience and its landscape and Living room wars. *Critical Studies in Mass Communication, 15*, 85- 90.

Juluri, V. (1998b). Why MTV digs India. *IndiaStar*. Available online: www.indiastar.com

Kaviraj, S. (1998). The culture of representative democracy. In P. Chatterjee (Ed.). *Wages of freedom: Fifty years of the Indian nation-state* (pp. 147–75). New Delhi: Oxford University Press.

Kaviraj, S. (1992). The imaginary institution of India. In P. Chatterjee & G. Pande (Eds.). *Subaltern studies 7: Writings on South Asian history and society* (pp. 1–39). New Delhi: Oxford University Press.

King, A. (1997). Introduction: Spaces of culture, spaces of knowledge. In A. King (Ed.). *Culture, globalization and the world system: Contemporary conditions for the representation of identity* (pp. 1–18). Minneapolis: University of Minnesota Press.

Kurien, C. (1994). *Global capitalism and the Indian economy*. Hyderabad, India: Orient Longman.

Lewis, J. (1994). The meaning of things. In J. Cruz & J. Lewis (Eds.). *Viewing, reading, listening: Audiences and cultural reception* (pp. 19–32). Boulder, CO: Westview.

Lewis, J. (1991). *The ideological octopus: An exploration of television and its audience.* New York: Routledge.

Lewis, J. (1983). The encoding/decoding model: Criticisms and developments for research on decoding. *Media, Culture and Society*, *5*, 151–69.

Liebes, T., & Katz, E. (1993). *The export of meaning: Cross-cultural readings of Dallas.* Cambridge, MA: Polity Press.

Livingstone, S. (1999). Mediated knowledge: Recognition of the familiar, discovery of the new. In J. Gripsrud (Ed.). *Television and common knowledge* (pp. 91–107). New York: Routledge.

Lunt, P., & Livingstone, S. (1996). Rethinking the focus group in media and communications research. *Journal of Communication*, *46*, 2, 79–97.

Lynch, O. (1990). The social construction of emotion in India. In O. Lynch (Ed.). *The social construction of emotion in India* (pp. 3–34). Berkeley: University of California Press.

Mankekar, P. (1999). *Screening culture, viewing politics: An ethnography of television, womanhood, and nation in postcolonial India.* Durham, NC: Duke University Press.

Manuel, P. (1993). *Cassette culture: Popular music and technology in North India.* Chicago: University of Chicago Press.

Martin-Barbero, J. (1993). *Communication, culture and hegemony: From the media to mediations* (E. Fox & R. White, Trans.). London: Sage.

McDowell, S. (1997). *Globalization, liberalization and policy change: A political economy of India's information sector.* New York: St. Martin's Press.

McKinley, E. (1997). *Beverly Hills 90210: Television, gender, and identity.* Philadelphia: University of Pennsylvania Press.

Mishra, V. (1998). *Devotional poetics and the Indian sublime.* Albany: State University of New York Press.

Morley, D. (1993). Active audience theory: Pendulums and pitfalls. *Journal of Communication*, *43*, 13–19.

Morley, D. (1980). *The 'nationwide audience': Structure and decoding.* London: British Film Institute.

Nandy, A. (1987). From outside the imperium: Gandhi's cultural critique of the West. In A. Nandy, *Traditions, tyrannies and utopias: Essays in the politics of awareness* (pp. 127–62). New Delhi: Oxford University Press.

Nandy, A. (1983). *The intimate enemy: Loss and recovery of self under colonialism.* Delhi: Oxford University Press.

Natrajan, B., & Parameswaran, R. (1997). Contesting the politics of ethnography: Towards an alternative knowledge production. *Journal of Communication Inquiry*, *21*, 27–59.

Nightingale, V. (1996). *Studying audiences: The shock of the real.* New York: Routledge.

Ninan, S. (1995). *Through the magic window: Television and change in India.* New Delhi: Penguin.

Ong, A. (1999). *Flexible citizenship: The cultural logics of transnationality*. Durham, NC: Duke University Press.

O'Sullivan, T., Hartley, J., Saunders, D., & Fiske, J. (1983). *Key concepts in communication*. New York: Routledge.

Pendakur, M., & Subramanyam, R. (1996). India: Indian cinema beyond national borders. In J. Sinclair, E. Jacka, & S. Cunningham (Eds.). *New patterns in global television* (pp. 67–81). New York: Oxford University Press.

Peters, J. (1993). Distrust of representation: Habermas on the public sphere. *Media, Culture & Society, 15*, 541–71.

Petras, J. (1993). Cultural imperialism in the late 20th century. *Journal of Contemporary Asia, 23*, 139–148.

Philo, G. (1999). MTV's global footprint. In R. Browne & M. Fishwick (Eds.). *Global village: Dead or alive?* (pp. 66–78). Bowling Green, OH: Bowling Green State University Press.

Radhakrishnan, R. (1994). Postmodernism and the rest of the world. *Organization, 1*, 305–340.

Rajagopal, A. (2000). Hindutva at play (interviewed by Darryl D' Monte). *Frontline*, 17. Available online: www.thehindu.com/frontline.

Ray, M., & Jacka, E. (1996). Indian television: An emerging regional force. In J. Sinclair, E. Jacka, & S. Cunningham (Eds). *New patterns in global television* (pp. 83–100). New York: Oxford University Press.

Roach, C. (1997). Cultural imperialism and resistance in media theory and literary theory. *Media, Culture & Society, 19*, 47–66.

Robertson, R. (1990). Mapping the global condition: Globalization as the central concept. *Theory, Culture, & Society*, 7, 15–30.

Rowell, L. (1992). *Music and musical thought in ancient India*. Chicago: University of Chicago Press.

Rudolph, L., & Rudolph, S. (1967). *The modernity of tradition: Political development in India*. Chicago: University of Chicago.

Said, E. (1978). *Orientalism*. New York: Vintage.

Schiller, H. (1991). Not yet the post-imperialist era. *Critical Studies in Mass Communication, 8*, 13–28.

Seiter, E. (1999). *Television and new media audiences*. New York: Oxford University Press.

Shah, A. (1997). *Hype, hypocricy and television in urban India*. New Delhi: Vikas.

Shepherd, J. (1986). Music consumption and cultural self-identities: Some theoretical and methodological reflections. *Media, Culture and Society, 8*, 305–30.

Stromer-Galley, J., & Schiappa, E. (1998). The argumentative burden of audience conjectures: Audience research in popular culture criticism. *Communication Theory, 8*, 1, 27–62.

Tagg, J. (1997). Globalization, totalization and the discursive field. In A. King (Ed.). *Culture, globalization and the world system: Contemporary conditions for the representation of identity* (pp. 154–160). Minneapolis: University of Minnesota Press.

Taylor, T. (1997). *Global pop: World music, world markets*. New York: Routledge.
Tomlinson, J. (1999). *Globalization and culture*. Chicago: University of Chicago Press.
Tomlinson, J. (1991). *Cultural imperialism: A critical introduction*. Baltimore: Johns Hopkins University Press.
Vaidyanathan, T. (1989). Authority and identity in India. *Daedalus, 118*, 147–69.
Waters, M. (1995). *Globalization*. New York: Routledge.
Wilson, R. & Dissanayake, W. (1996). *Global/Local: Cultural production and the transnational imaginary*. Durham, NC: Duke University Press.
Yadava, J. (1999). Trends in mass communication in 21st century. *Yojana*, 10–14.
Yoshimoto, M. (1996). Real virtuality. In R. Wilson & W. Dissanayake (Eds.). *Global/Local: Cultural production and the transnational imaginary*. Durham, NC: Duke University Press.

Nonacademic Periodicals

As most of the original addresses for many of the on-line sources listed here may have changed, I provide the main addresses in a separate list that follows.

Agarwal, A. (1996, January 31). From rock bottom to top ten. *India Today*, 96–99.
Agarwal, A. & Mukhopadhyay, P. (1997, July 6–12). Doordarshan rules, OK? *Sunday*, 18–26.
Annuncio, C. (1997, July 23). The discovery of India. *Outlook*, 51–55.
Arathoon, M. (2000, April 19–24). What after MTV? NTV, stupid. *The Economic Times* [on-line].
Arathoon, M. (1997, December 17–23). Caught napping. *The Economic Times* [online].
Bhatia, S. (1997, August 9). The song of freedom. *The Telegraph Weekend*, 1.
Bijapurkar, R. (1998, March 4–10). A market in discontinuity. *The Economic Times* [on-line].
Brijnath, R., & Chopra, A. (1997, September 1). Vande Mataram: A song for India. *India Today*, 54–55.
Chatterjee, S. (1997, June 18). Heavyweight measures. *Outlook*, 64–66.
Chaya, R. (1997, December 19). Branding for success. *Screen* [on-line].
Chopra, A. (1997, March 15). A musical explosion. *India Today*, 80–82.
Chopra, A. (1997, August 4). Popcorn artist. *India Today*, 81.
"Couch potatoes on the rise." (1998, February 13). *Screen* [on-line].
Chougule, A. (2000 September 29). Sing a song for a crore. *Screen* [on-line].
D'Souza, V. (1992, October 11). Desperately seeking Sudha. *The Week*, 16–18.
Elsham, R. (2002, March 22). Huge growth seen for Indian TV revenue. *India West*, B 8.
"Etc." (2001, August 24). *Screen* [on-line].
Ghose, S., & Jahagirdar, A. (1998, December 1–14). Trendy conservatives: Cool in Kaliyug. *Outlook*, 61–70.

"Global village unplugged." (1998, January 2). *Screen* [online].
Govardan, D. (1999, January 7). Sun TV plans North American foray with Sunworld TV. *The Economic Times* [on-line].
Hassan, N. (1997, June 13–19). Tight purse. *The Andhra Pradesh Times Leisure*, 8–9.
Hassan, N. (1997, August 8–14). TRP's: Popularity conflict. *The Andhra Pradesh Times Leisure*. 6–7.
Hussain, S. (1999, February 10–16). There's something about attitude. *The Economic Times* [on-line].
Hussain, S. (1999, March 3–9). Finetuning. *The Economic Times* [on-line].
Hussain, S. (1997, August 6–12). V' Jaying on. *The Economic Times*, 8.
"It's open war." (1997, November 7). *Screen* [on-line].
Iyengar, P. (1994, June 12). Hyderabad braces for megacity status. *The Times of India*, 7.
Iyer, L. (1997, May 25). The cyber rush. *The Week*, 50–51.
Kohli, V. (1997, January 15). For the love of self. *Advertising & Marketing*, 61–62.
Madhav, K. (2002, April 3). Timeless appeal. *The Hindu* [on-line].
"Major shift in TV viewership." (1997, November 14). *Screen* [on-line].
McCaughan, D. (1998, March 4–10). Hanging out? That's cool! *The Economic Times* [on-line].
Moses, K. (1995). Selling songs through TV. *Deccan Chronicle*, 17.
Mukherjee, R. (1998, February 25-March 3). Cable stable. *The Economic Times* [on-line].
Mukherjee, R. (1997, July 15–21). The sound of music, Sony style. *The Economic Times* [on-line].
Mukherjee, R. (1997, May 23). Music cos changing their tunes to survive. *The Economic Times*, 7.
Mukherjee, R. & Hussain, S. (1997, November 19–25). When two's not company. *The Economic Times* [on-line].
"Music Asia claims to be No 1 music channel." (1997, November 1). *The Economic Times* [on-line].
"Music is mantra at B4U." (2001, August 17). *Screen* [on-line].
"Music Mania!" (1998, July 8–14). *The Economic Times* [on-line].
Naik, N., & Karani, N. (1997, July 18–24). Countdown to success. *The Andhra Pradesh Times Leisure*, 8–9.
"A peek into rural TV viewership." (1997, November 28). *Screen* [on-line].
Pinto, J. (1997, June 16). In sync with the audience. *The Times of India*, 3.
Rao, Ch. (1997, May 8). Move to collect entry fee; Standoff between studios, TV channels. *Andhra Pradesh Times*, 1.
Rawla, B., & Hussain, S. (1997, October 15–21). MTV renewed. *The Economic Times* [on-line].
Sahai, P. (1997, May). The great gig in the sky. *Advertising & Marketing*, 42–51.
Sehgal, R. (1997, August 3). Ridge Forrester just can't speak Hindi. *The Sunday Times of India Review*, 1.

Sethi, V. (1997, August 8–14). India, mon amour. *The Andhra Pradesh Times Leisure*, 8–9.

Sharan, A., & Hussain, S. (1997, May 14–20). Copycat Muqabla. *The Economic Times*, 1.

Singh, G. (1999, January 9). Channel V to take on rival MTV on US turf. *The Economic Times* [on-line].

"Sony accused of defacing Krishna." (1997, April 10). *Asian Age*, 1.

Tellis, B., & Frank, M. (1996, December 1). India goes pop! *Femina*, pp. 14–24.

"Tellybuzz." (1997, September 6). *Screen* [on-line].

"Tussle at the top." (1997, November 21). *Screen* [on-line].

Unnikrishnan, C. (2002, March 29-April 4). Comedy is a serious business. *Screen* [on-line].

Vesuna, S. (1995, November 19). Serial killers. *The Week*, 64–65.

Wagle, J. (1997, August 1). The booming business of music videos. *Screen*, 33.

On-Line Source Addresses

The Economic Times. Available www.economictimes.com

The Hindu. Available www.the-hindu.com

Screen. Available www.expressindia.com/screen

The Times of India. Available www.timesofindia.com

INDEX

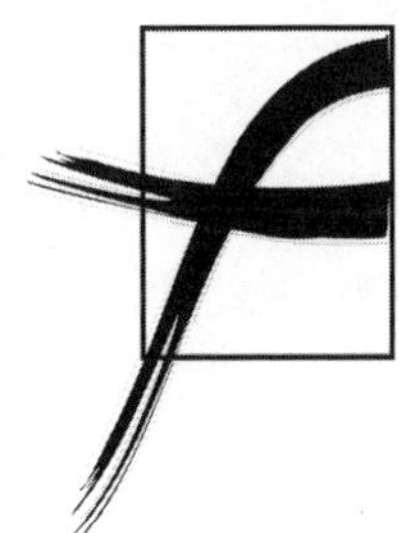

Intersections in Communications and Culture

Global Approaches and Transdisciplinary Perspectives

General Editors: Cameron McCarthy & Angharad N. Valdivia

An Institute of Communications Research, University of Illinois Commemorative Series

This series aims to publish a range of new critical scholarship that seeks to engage and transcend the disciplinary isolationism and genre confinement that now characterizes so much of contemporary research in communication studies and related fields. The editors are particularly interested in manuscripts that address the broad intersections, movement, and hybrid trajectories that currently define the encounters between human groups in modern institutions and societies and the way these dynamic intersections are coded and represented in contemporary popular cultural forms and in the organization of knowledge. Works that emphasize methodological nuance, texture and dialogue across traditions and disciplines (communications, feminist studies, area and ethnic studies, arts, humanities, sciences, education, philosophy, etc.) and that engage the dynamics of variation, diversity and discontinuity in the local and international settings are strongly encouraged.

LIST OF TOPICS

- Multidisciplinary Media Studies
- Cultural Studies
- Gender, Race, & Class
- Postcolonialism
- Globalization
- Diaspora Studies
- Border Studies
- Popular Culture
- Art & Representation
- Body Politics
- Governing Practices
- Histories of the Present
- Health (Policy) Studies
- Space and Identity
- (Im)migration
- Global Ethnographies
- Public Intellectuals
- World Music
- Virtual Identity Studies
- Queer Theory
- Critical Multiculturalism

Manuscripts should be sent to:

Cameron McCarthy OR Angharad N. Valdivia
Institute of Communications Research
University of Illinois at Urbana-Champaign
222B Armory Bldg., 555 E. Armory Avenue
Champaign, IL 61820